# Anti-Aging *and* Secrets *of* Healthy Living *to* Stop *the* Clock!

*Learn how to look younger, feel fantastic and wow the world!*

MARY-BETH NEWELL, RN, MS

*This book is dedicated to the many lovely ladies I have met over the years who repeatedly asked me, "Whatare you doing?" and then after I would answer, replied, "You should write a book".*

# Table of Contents

# INTRODUCTION

You might be wondering why I wrote this book and how it might be different from other health and wellness books. Every girl has hobbies she really enjoys. Health, wellness, and beauty have always been areas of fascination for me. I had two older sisters, seven and nine years my senior, and as a young child I was captivated by watching them prepare for dates and dances. They had a collection of lotions, potions, and curlers that made them look absolutely glowing and beautiful to my mind. Who wouldn't be intrigued by the magic of beauty?!

Over the years, I have experimented with several ways to stop the aging clock or at least slow it down. This is one clock that you are fine with being a little slow! I prefer natural methods to maintain my youth and I have tried a lot. Some were duds, but other methods are clear winners that I will share with you. I try to avoid putting toxins or chemicals in my body or relying on plastic surgery. Unfortunately, I've seen too many plastic surgery mishaps that cannot be fixed. While there are very talented surgeons, plastic surgery does come with risks and a high price tag. I'm a girl who is willing to put in the work to achieve lasting results!

It isn't just what you do to the outside of your body that matters, but also how you treat the inside. Nutrition, exercise, and how you see the world all matter more than you may realize. There are strong connections that we'll explore, and some things may surprise you! Other books may discuss theories and topics in an esoteric way. I'll share real-life examples of what to do and mistakes to avoid!

Whether you are looking for a few tips to improve yourself or want a complete overhaul, this is the book for you! It is packed with information to enhance your appearance, feel more positive, and improve your health. I appreciate value and am a DIY-er. There are so many inexpensive, high-value things we can do to improve our health, feel great, and really shine from within. As a busy and budget-conscious woman, I know how challenging it can be to incorporate new processes or products into your daily routine. That is exactly why I have given tips on how you can incorporate these practices into your life. My goal is for you to learn something new, feel energized, and be the most beautiful woman you can be – inside and out!

# EXERCISE

# What's the Big Deal about Strength Training?

You hear it all the time, "You need to do strength training," but why? You know it helps to tone and that weight-bearing exercise is good for the bones, but is it really a big deal? Yes, it is and can lead to a healthier and longer life! Strength training, especially high-intensity strength training, can prevent cognitive decline and boost brain power. Goodbye, brain fog! Do you want a natural antianxiety remedy? Yes, strength training with moderate to heavy weights has been clinically proven to reduce anxiety and release endorphins that combat depressive feelings. It can improve sleep too. Really? Yes, by reducing the aches and stiffness many people get, you'll have a more restful night of sleep.

Okay, this sounds good. Anything else? Yes, strength training not only builds muscle but helps the muscle take in and utilize glucose contributing to better blood sugar levels. This is great news for people with type 2 diabetes. We've all heard that belly fat is bad. Belly fat is associated with an increase in cardiovascular issues and cancer. It releases proteins and hormones that cause inflammation, and we all know that inflammation is not good.

You can reduce belly fat or visceral fat with strength training, and not only will you look better, but you will also reduce your cardiovascular and cancer risk. It takes time, but you will see the results. Although I was within an ideal BMI range, my tummy was not well defined. I started doing strength training and core exercises for about eight minutes a day and within five months I had transformed my abdominal muscles. Eight minutes a day is doable for the incredible benefits that can be achieved.

Interestingly, strength training also influences your self-image. Whether you are actually getting well-defined muscles or not, women who did strength training perceived their bodies as being more attractive. This could be the result of an increase in endorphins, a clearer mind, or feeling more energetic. Whatever the reason, I'll take it! Who doesn't want to feel better about themselves?

Other benefits include increased flexibility, balance, and range of motion. Have you tried doing a split recently or reaching to touch your toes with your legs extended? Remember how effortless it was to do these things as a child? Well, strength training may not put you at an Olympic level of flexibility and mobility, but it can lengthen your muscles. The ultimate result is a reduced risk of injury. Strength training increases the amount and diameter of collagen in your tendons to keep you strong and on the move! I am a marathon runner and after consistently doing my strength training, I was amazed at how much EASIER it was to complete a run, and my recovery time was minimal!

I mentioned it helps to promote healthy bones and prevent osteoporosis. Who wants Swiss cheese bones that can snap like a twig? I can attest that strength training works. Throughout my life if I could walk instead of drive, I have done so. I specifically select practitioners, pharmacies, beauticians, etc., within walking distance so I can get extra exercise. I multi-task when brushing my teeth by doing squats and lunges. I have been known to strap on some ankle and wrist weights while working around the house or taking the dogs for a walk. I am a busy girl and need to maximize my time! Well, the effort and my love of dairy products has paid off. My DEX scan report said I had the bones of a twenty-five-year-old! Even if your bones are not going back in time, you can preserve and improve them with strength training.

Women are usually very focused on cardio exercises to maintain their figures, burn calories and improve their cardiovascular health. We need to be just as focused on strength training. Strength training burns calories during and after your workouts. You might not realize that people with greater muscle mass burn more calories! You're sold and you are asking how long you must do it? Studies indicate that as little as thirty to sixty minutes a week can give you life extending benefits.

You want to exercise your major muscle groups so select a variety of exercises and you can divide your strength training into as few as two or three days during the week. If you can't make it to the gym, search for YouTube videos. (My favorite is the "8 Minute" series with Jamie Brenkus. They are an oldie but a goodie and do they ever work miracles!) Or develop your own routine with weights. Wherever and however you do it, know that you are significantly improving your health and that is DEFINITELY something you can feel good about!

## Use It or Lose It

We've all heard the term "Use It or Lose It" and it can apply to several things: a foreign language, sports, or maintaining your muscles. Exercise is SO important for good mental health, cognition, weight control, and strong muscles and bones. The key is consistency.

Everyone, including myself, has gotten the "exercise bug" and gone gangbusters, and later your routine drops off and becomes a distant memory. You may feel guilty about not exercising or upset you cannot find time. Well, where there is a will there is a way, ladies! This is a MUST DO and you CAN incorporate it into even the most hectic of schedules. And not to worry, I am going to help you with ideas on how to make sure you get that much-needed exercise every day.

First, you need to commit to exercising. That tends to be the easier part rather than actually finding the time to do it. For me, I KNOW I need to exercise. If I don't, I get VERY crabby and begin to not like being around myself. My ideal is a good sixty to ninety minutes of exercise time a day. An hour on the treadmill or walking the dogs, then strength training for another fifteen minutes or so. It is heaven! Yet, I have those days where it is almost all I can do to get through the day. A few of those days and look out!

So, what do I do to try and maintain my own mental health (and that of those around me)? Here are my "go-to" Plan B ideas. If I know or even suspect I may have a crazy busy day, I start out by doing squats or leg lifts while brushing my teeth. I use an electric toothbrush so it will be two minutes in the morning and two minutes at night. I figure four minutes is better than no minutes. If I am at home and busy around the house, I sometimes strap leg weights to my ankles and light bracelet-type weights to my wrists. It is extra energy expended and helps with strength training.

If I am out and about, I use these tips to get some steps in. Park as far away as you can from the entrance of a building. Take the steps instead of an elevator. Hey, you say you must go to the 8th floor! No problem, take the elevator to the 7th floor and walk up a flight. Walk down two flights and catch the down elevator on the 6th floor. In fact, a good practice for every day is to use the stairs if you are going down two flights or up one flight. Walk the stairs on the escalator instead of standing for the ride.

Pace or walk around while you are on the phone. You will be surprised how many steps you can get in during a ten-minute phone call. Of course, this doesn't always work if you need to be on camera or checking your computer, but we all have calls that don't require us to be "on" at least part of the day. I got 4000 steps in while waiting for customer service as I was pacing angrily around my house. I was so frustrated, I needed to do SOMETHING while I waited. I was surprised by how many steps I got. It also helped to dissipate some of my crabbiness, so I didn't snap at the representative.

Do a few squats when you use the restroom. Walk around the house as you are checking your social media. Scrolling through Facebook can surprisingly eat up a big chunk of time. Multi-task by looking at social media and getting some steps in! I try to find all my "providers" (beauty, medical, pharmacy, etc.) within a mile of my house. Why? So, I can walk or bike to my appointments instead of driving. A five-minute walk back and forth adds up to a ten-minute walk.

Even getting in an abbreviated workout is better than none. If I only have thirty minutes, I may not go to the gym but rather jog or walk around the neighborhood. And don't forget that you may have ALREADY gotten exercise in, albeit in non-traditional forms. Did you mow the grass? Clean your house? Garden or weed for an hour? Went to Costco to shop and walked a few miles? Yes, yes I did! Good for you.

As I said before, "Use It or Lose It." You CAN fit exercise in and if you get bored with the "same old, same old" routine, then mix it up with something fun. How about dancing? Whether you go out to a venue or shake it up at home, dancing is fun! Do you like to swim? Uh, somewhat. Well, you might not do fifty laps, but how about a water exercise class or maybe pool volleyball? Not into vigorous exercise? What about yoga? You'd be surprised how many muscle groups you work in a yoga session. Or commit yourself to "window shopping" at a mall for an hour. Remember that any walking is better than no walking.

Many animal shelters have a program where you can take a dog for a day or half day. The idea is for the dog to get out in the fresh air and exercise. It's fun exercise for you too while also doing a good deed! Look into community hiking or walking groups. Meet Up is a great way to find out what is in your area. For the more active gal, consider signing up for a run. Challenge yourself so you'll need to train for the event for several weeks or months. You've done a 5k, now tackle a 10k. You ran 13.1 miles, how about 26.2? If you aren't into longer distances, consider training to improve your "personal best." The benefits, both mental and physical, that you get from exercise cannot be overstated.

## I Don't Like Beer, But I Want a Six-Pack!

Are you feeling a little like the Pillsbury dough boy? You've gotten your tummy flat or fairly flat but there is no definition. You're dying to wear that bikini and give up the one piece but aren't sure what to do to get at least a four-pack. There are exercises to tighten the tummy once you're at your ideal weight or start doing them on your weight-loss journey.

Now, not all girls will be able to get the chiseled six-pack no matter how hard they try. Some of the "out of your control" factors include genetics and how you store fat. The apple body type tends to store fat around the middle. If you have that body type, it will be harder to see the six-pack level of definition as it is dependent on the amount of subcutaneous fat stored in your abdomen. You also need to have a lower percentage of body fat. For women, this range is between 16–20%. You could have a higher percentage of body fat and be healthy. You can still get a toned tummy with core-strengthening exercises and look really good!

So, whether you desire the six-pack or just a sexy toned tummy, core exercises are the key. Not only do these exercises help you look better, but there are also other benefits too! One study showed that after four weeks of training the ability to catch yourself and stand up when you are about to fall improved. Another study with college runners showed improvement in static balance, endurance, and running performance after eight weeks of training. Are you having back pain? Core training to the rescue!

To be effective, core training only needs to take place two to three times a week. If you can do more, go for it! You want exercises that involve side-to-side, forward, backward, and twisting movements. These may include various crunches, plank exercises, and other "lifting" exercises. There are videos on YouTube that offer a plethora of options. I like the "8 Minute Abs" by Jaime Brenkus and do my exercises every other day. His video includes all three types of movements, is fun, and has a countdown timer (Yes, only ten more seconds of this movement!). The only additional exercises that I find beneficial are plank movements and exercises using a medicine ball. I also consciously hold my stomach in while sitting at my desk or walking the dogs. I figure every little bit helps! Be patient, it took some time before I saw impressive results.

Besides the core-strengthening exercises, being focused on nutrition, sleep, and fat-burning exercises will help you achieve your goals. Cardio exercise is great for burning fat. Whether it is walking fast, running, or doing a video in front of the TV, you'll want to keep your heart healthy, mind clear, and body trim. Protein is key for muscle development so be sure you are getting enough protein. It also fills you up and keeps you satisfied. Fiber moves slowly through the digestive system, so you feel full longer and will be less likely to snack.

Refined carbohydrates can derail any nutrition or physical fitness plan. Refined carbohydrates include processed foods, bakery goodies, and pasta. Do your best to avoid these as much as you can. If you MUST have a cookie, seek out low-carb versions from Adkins or other manufacturers. Dying for a plate of spaghetti? Go for the whole wheat noodles. And stay hydrated! Your muscles will thank you, and you'll feel SO much better. Many times, when people are feeling the 3 pm slump (You know, you are getting tired and hungry), you are just dehydrated. No need for a piece of candy or a cup of coffee. Try a tall drink of water and most times, your energy will be restored!

## Ahh, It Feels SO Good to Stretch!

I think kitties have it all figured out. Have you ever watched a kitty STRETCH itself out and YOU feel good watching it? Stretching is a vitally important activity that often gets overlooked because it doesn't burn calories. But stretching keeps our muscles flexible and strong, can reduce those aches and pains and improve our posture!

Other benefits include reducing stress. When you are stressed, your muscles are stressed too. Do you suffer from tension headaches? Stretching can reduce stress and tension, helping to reduce or minimize those annoying headaches. Yes, you can achieve some Zen by stretching it out! Combine your activity with meditation or listening to "spa" music to get double duty out of your routine.

Stretching is an activity that needs to be done five to ten minutes several times a week and it may take months to see quantifiable results, but it is worth it! There are two main types of stretching: dynamic and static. Dynamic stretches warm up your muscles and prepare them for movement. These are perfect as a pre-workout routine. Dynamic sounds like active and these are active stretches. Examples include arm circles, lunges, and trunk rotations. After doing these, I think, "I am ready to go!" Your muscles will be ready to go too. What about Pilates three times a week, is that dynamic stretching? Yes, if you are already doing Pilates then you are doing dynamic stretching exercises that also focus on toning.

Static stretches are exercises where you are holding a position for ten to thirty seconds. These stretches are beneficial after you exercise to reduce the risk of injury. Examples include holding your arm across your chest or reaching for your toes and holding the position. I call these my "ahh" stretches. They feel SO good after exercising when you just want to relax afterwards. Does yoga count as stretching? Yoga includes holding static stretches but goes beyond just stretching. It has other components such as breathing, strength training, and more of a focus on mindfulness. If you have never done yoga, you realize very quickly that it is not an "easy" exercise. If you are just starting out, I'd recommend a stretching routine and not yoga. Get comfortable with stretching before diving into yoga.

What if you are not into exercising? You can still perform stretching activities to improve flexibility and feel good. It is easy to find a stretching routine. YouTube has a wide variety. To get the benefit of a calm mind look for routines that incorporate mindfulness. You can download a stretching guide that outlines various stretches. You can easily incorporate your stretches while watching the news in the morning or TV in the evening. If you have a desk job, you can take a break and do five to ten minutes of stretching exercises, and you'll feel oh so refreshed when you return to your desk! It is better than a cup of coffee or a candy bar.

A few tips if you are starting a routine. Check in with your practitioner if you have an existing injury or have physical limitations where certain stretches might be contraindicated. Avoid bouncing and don't go past the point of feeling some tension. The phrase "no pain, no gain" doesn't apply here. If you feel discomfort or pain, you need to back off a bit. Don't stretch cold muscles. You want to be a hottie! Warm up with a walk or a few minutes on the treadmill before performing pre-workout stretches. Once you've started a stretching routine you are going to be hooked! It is such a luxurious way to improve flexibility, reduce injury, and look younger with your improved posture!

## Track It and Trend It

I am a very goal-oriented person and love checking things off my "To Do" list. I am motivated by setting a target and meeting it. A fitness tracker is a great motivator for me. I like the ease of having my steps, miles, calories, sleep quality, and more tracked for me. I can look at how I am doing during the day, week, month, or even compared to years ago! I especially find the number of hours I sleep and quality to be beneficial. You can see the impact on sleep quality if you had a couple of glasses of wine the night before (The numbers are pretty dismal), spent the hour before retiring scrolling through your Facebook page (Blue light does not promote the best sleep), did high-intensity exercise in the evening (Getting revved up doesn't result in restful sleep) or if you disengaged from electronics at least an hour before sleep (It DOES lead to better sleep).

Tracking your progress, whether by using a fitness journal, log, or fitness tracker results in more consistent workouts. I have been taking my measurements for years. I have a log of my calf, thigh, hip, tummy, breast, and upper arm measurements along with my weight. All you need is a piece of paper, a pen, and measuring tape. I periodically check my measurements. Sometimes my weight does not change, but my measurements improve as I am developing my muscles (muscle tissue weighs more than fat).

Some girls like to take a "before" picture in a bikini of their front, back, and side profile, then take other pictures throughout their journey to see how their bodies are changing. Another way I stay motivated is to use a paper calendar for the month where I record my strength training sessions. It is rewarding to write down "abs" or "buns" after I complete a session. I also track how many weeks I have been doing it.

Monitoring trends can provide a wealth of information! My trend shows that I am MUCH more active in June and July than the rest of the year. It must be the longer days and great weather! I can also see from years of tracking how my weight has changed. I've been pleased that it has gone down and stabilized, although I can see trends every year where it climbs a little in November and December. Okay, so maybe the time change with darker days, holiday cookies, and cocktail parties might have something to do with it. My sister has a great initiative that she does every year. She calls it "maintain, not gain." The idea is to weigh yourself the week before Thanksgiving and then after the New Year with a goal to maintain your weight and not gain any pounds.

Another trend I've noticed is when I REALLY up my exercise I tend to gain weight. Wait, what is happening? For me, there is a sweet spot where I burn calories and maintain my weight. If I overexercise, my appetite goes into overdrive. I can do an extra hour of cardio if needed, but if I ramp it up for a week, I become ravenous and end up gaining weight (and no, it is not all muscle). Sleep is so important, and I can see how my sleep quality changes based on the number of hours I slept, as well as reflecting on any activities I did the evening before. What trends will you find?

# Do I Really Need 10,000 Steps a Day?

Who decided that 10,000 steps a day was optimal? Was it based on research or a consensus of medical professionals? No, it was a marketing idea for a pedometer back in 1964! 10,000 steps equal approximately five miles. The average American walks between 3,000 and 4,000 steps a day or about 1.5–2 miles.

What does the US Department of Health and Human Services recommend? They recommend 150 minutes a week of moderately intense exercise. Examples of moderate intensity are brisk walking, walking upstairs, cleaning, mowing the grass, doubles tennis (or pickleball), and riding your bike. You may already be doing a lot of those activities during the week! The 150 minutes can be broken up throughout the week. Some girls might devote thirty minutes a day to walking Fido, other girls may clean for fifteen minutes a day, and play pickleball for forty-five minutes one day a week. If you have a big yard, you may get half your minutes just by mowing the grass!

Now, if you average thirty minutes of moderate-intensity exercise a week, you won't average 10,000 steps a day. So, is there a benefit to getting more steps? Let's look at thresholds where you see benefits. If you get at least 2,700 steps a day, your risk of death is decreased by 8%, and if you can average 9,000 steps a day, your risk of dying early is reduced by 60%! Cardiovascular events are decreased by 11% getting 2,700 steps but are reduced by 51% if you average 7,000 steps a day. Your risk for developing diabetes, high blood pressure, and obesity is reduced as well!

Wow, you're wondering where you can get your fitness tracker? Check out your phone, many include a pedometer feature. Other options include a wearable fitness tracker that can be basic or fancy. High-end versions may allow you to get your emails and text messages. While you do not necessarily need 10,000 steps a day to see these health benefits, walking 10,000 steps a day is an effective way to reduce or maintain an ideal weight and get your exercise. There are other benefits such as releasing feel good hormones, reducing the risk of depression, and improving sleep.

If you are at the 3,000–4,000 steps average and want to increase to the sweet spot of 9,000 steps, how do you do it? Using a fitness tracker or old-fashioned pedometer is a great motivator. If I am at the low end of my goal at the end of the day, I will up my activity after dinner with a brisk walk. Other times, I am AMAZED at how many steps I can get if I am cleaning the house and doing laundry. Who knew all that running around easily gets you to 10,000 steps?! No wonder we are tired after a day of active chores!

Aim to increase your average steps by 1,000 a day each week. You won't get burned out, and it is a nice transition to moving up to 9,000 steps or more. Think about how you can add steps; select the parking spot farthest away from the store. Not only will it be easy to find a space, but your car is also less likely to get "dinged" and you'll probably get an extra 500 steps in. Yes, it is a can-do! Other ways of getting your steps in include dancing to tunes. Or going for a short walk after dinner. Not only will you give your food time to digest and avoid seconds, but you'll also get some fresh air!

If you work in an office, instead of sending your colleague an email walk over to their desk to collaborate. Ditch the elevator and take the steps to go to lunch. If you work on the tenth floor, get off the elevator on the 8th floor, and walk up! Desk jobs can be a killer for getting your steps. Set an alarm and take a short walk every hour or two. Not only will it help your vision by getting away from the computer for five minutes, but you'll also feel less fatigued as the day goes on. One study reported that people who exercised for an hour a day but sat for thirteen and a half hours or more a day did not see any health benefits. So, let's get moving!

## Ladies Who Hunch

You've heard of "ladies who lunch", which can be social and fun. You definitely don't want to be one of the "ladies that hunch!" I had a good friend who looked at me one day and said, "You are hunching your shoulders, and it makes you look old." And here, I thought I had good posture until I looked in the mirror we were passing by. Then I saw the forward hunch as I was walking and could only envision how it would progress and what I would look like in twenty years. Not the look I was hoping for!

Not only does poor posture make us look older, but it also causes other health issues. Poor posture can lead to a pot belly, muscle pain, fatigue, and impaired balance. As if that isn't enough, poor posture can lead to stress incontinence as it increases abdominal pressure and reduces the effect of the pelvic floor muscles. The increase in abdominal pressure can slow the digestive process and lead to heartburn. By now, you've probably run to the mirror to check your posture and might be saying, "Uh oh, my shoulders are hunching!"

Poor posture can be corrected in most cases. There are exercises to strengthen and lengthen your shoulders and upper back. These include chin tucks, shoulder blade pinches, bird dogs, and dumbbell squats. Chin tucks are where you stand upright and pull your head and neck back, hold for a few seconds, and repeat. It keeps your head aligned with your spine. Shoulder blade pinches, thankfully, don't involve anyone actually pinching you, rather you stand with your arms held upright at a ninety-degree angle and move them towards your back "pinching" your shoulder blades. These feel good! A bird-dog exercise is where you get on all fours, then extend your right arm and left leg out and hold the position. You look like a hunting dog when it sees a bird. This exercise helps to develop correct posture and keep the spine in alignment. Dumbbell squats involve holding a weight while doing squats. They help with developing strength and maintaining good posture! You can incorporate these into your daily routine, and some can be done when you are in your car!

I sit at a desk for a good part of the day. While I strive to sit with my back straight, it takes focus to not be a huncher. A tip is to set an alarm or set a time to look at yourself in a mirror or consciously check your posture. As you look in the mirror, move your shoulders back, lift your chest, and hold your head high. You will feel taller and breathe better! Once you are aware of what "good posture" feels like, you won't even need to look in a mirror to know if you are slouching. To help make this position a habit, invest in a posture corrector. Yes, they do make such things. They are inexpensive and can be worn anywhere from fifteen minutes to two hours. Some bra manufacturers have designed their brassieres to help with your posture as well, although they tend to be more heavy-duty models.

Other invaluable tips include keeping items at eye level. Think about how much time you spend looking down at your phone scrolling through social media, shopping, or researching recipes. You might want to use your posture corrector while you scroll! A contoured pillow can help to keep your neck and back in alignment. Unfortunately, they aren't made with down feathers and might take a while to acclimate if you are a fan of down pillows.

Osteoporosis contributes to fractures that can be a cause of kyphosis (a hunchback). Ensure you are taking in enough calcium and vitamin D in your diet or supplement your diet if you need to do so. You want to keep your bones strong! I love dairy products and while I am not twenty-five years old, my last bone scan reported I had the bones of a twenty-five-year-old. And don't forget about protein.

Protein is the building block for muscle development, and we want strong muscles to keep us upright! If you aren't a big fan of meat and beans in your diet, there are yummy shakes and bars to get your protein in. The earlier you start focusing on your posture, the easier it will be to correct and maintain. The next time I see my friend, I'm sure she WON'T be telling me that I'm hunching my shoulders!

## What Happened to My Butt and How Can I Get It Back?

If you are older than twenty-five you probably have noticed some changes to your derriere. That perky, perfect butt might be a bit saggy. It is natural for our gluteal muscles to atrophy a bit as we get older. We are not running around all day playing outside like we did as children or walking all over the place as college kids. We're adults who are working and spending a lot more time sitting in the car or at a desk.

The average female loses 5% of muscle mass every ten years starting at thirty-five years old. One study found that at eighty years old, people lost up to 50% of their muscle mass. Yikes! We have no time to waste. Another fun way to evaluate perkiness is the pencil test. It helps you know if you are getting a saggy butt. You place a pencil in the crease where the bottom of your derriere meets your leg. If the pencil drops, you have a perky behind! If it stays in place or disappears, then you may want to start a program to perk it up!

Some girls may want to lose a few pounds. Excess fat adds weight and can weaken the gluteal muscles, which results in sagginess. If you are going to start slimming down, note that rapid weight loss contributes further to a droopy bottom. Slower weight loss makes it easier for your body to adjust to the changes. All girls can benefit from a healthy diet. Avoid processed foods and refined carbohydrates. I think we've all heard "A moment on the lips, a lifetime on the hips." No one can be perfect all the time but trying to make wise food choices or switching to "better for you" options most of the time will definitely help. I love the "Eat This, Not That" series of books that provide tasty options for high-fat, high-sugar, or high-calorie foods. And keep in mind that protein is needed to build muscle and improve skin elasticity.

You say you're ready for exercise, and are asking what you should do? We all know that in real estate, it is location, location, location. Well with the behind it is squat, squat, squat. Squats are the single best exercise. Be sure you are performing a squat correctly. A squat is when you get into a sitting position, stand up, and sit back down. Look in the mirror to be sure you are in good form. You don't want to be doing them and injure yourself or not see any results.

If you are just getting started, you might want to sit in a chair and stand for several repetitions. Squats are not my favorite, but they are a must-do! I try to incorporate them into my daily routine. I use an electric toothbrush that has a two-minute timer. And you guessed it, I do squats for two minutes in the morning and, usually, in the evening too. Easy, peasy way to get the dreaded squats in. Besides squats, you want to keep those legs moving!

I walk everywhere I can and if I must drive somewhere, I park far away. Get those steps in! Stairs are your friend. Jump on the stair master at the gym. No time for the gym? Forget the elevator or escalator and climb the stairs. Even a few floors will help if you can't walk up five stories. Do you live in a two-story house? Lucky you! You can climb the stairs every day! Or create your own "step" at home with a milk crate or buy a "step" from E-bay or Amazon. Do you like the outdoors? Join a hiking group or venture out on your own.

Other exercises that help you get a better butt include fire hydrants. This seems like such a silly exercise. You get on all fours, lift your leg to the side like a dog and hold, lower and repeat on the other side. Your dog may start looking at you quizzically wondering what you are doing. For added oomph, add some leg weights. A glute bridge is fun too. Lying on your back with your feet flat and bent knees, lift those hips keeping your weight on your heels. Dead lifts seem so simple but work. Lunges are another go-to exercise for a prettier derriere. Do you mean to get your exercises in but need some motivation? Search YouTube for butt-exercise videos. I personally like Jaime Brenkus' "8 Minute Buns." I've also tried the Brazilian Butt Lift. Both keep you motivated and are uplifting (pun intended). For more drastic results, you can consult with a plastic surgeon, although, I'd recommend trying the DIY route first!

Now that we've covered ways to get toned and keep our bodies moving for improved health, let's move on to how we can get glowing and younger-looking skin!

# SKIN CARE and MORE

## Create a Home Spa – Set the Tone!

Who doesn't love pampering? So why not treat yourself at home?! It is easy and budget-friendly to create your own private retreat to refresh and revitalize yourself. So how do you create this oasis? First, select some soothing tunes. If you Google "spa music," you will find many free options that you can play from your phone. There are options from three to twelve hours! You can "upgrade" and attach a speaker to your phone or use noise-cancelling headphones. I love my mini Bluetooth speaker that produces a big sound!

Next, let's get the aromatherapy going. Easy options are candles or a diffuser. Candles come in a variety of scents. "Fresh Linen" or "Ocean" might do the trick. Lavender- and eucalyptus-scented candles can also aid in the relaxation experience. Essential oils are another option and are used in a diffuser. There are essential oils for every mood, but we want to Zen out! Lavender is known for its relaxation properties, and you could just use a few drops of lavender in a diffuser.

If you want to really replicate the spa experience, get a "spa day only" robe. You know the one I am talking about – white, oversized, soft, and cuddly! If you do not already have one, you can search for one online. They average about $100, so it might be something you put on your wish list or drop a hint that it might make a nice birthday or holiday gift. It is a perfect gift that several people could "go in on."

Pour yourself a glass of wine, sparkling water, or a soothing, relaxing tea. The choice is yours! Or create your own flavored water. Cucumber water is easy to make and so incredibly refreshing. Thinly slice a cucumber, place the slices in a pitcher with water, and chill. In a few hours, you will not have to worry about hydrating enough. It is almost impossible not to keep drinking this delicious water!

# Create a Home Spa – Let the Beautification Begin

Okay, so now we've got the mood set. Let's get to the beauty treatments! What are you in the mood for? A facial, creating a lustrous head of hair, or a mani-pedi? We can do it all! A great facial starts with thoroughly cleansing your face and opening your pores with steam. Use a luxurious face wash. A cream-based cleanser feels wonderful.

If you have invested in a face brush, use it to deep clean your face. They do a great job of exfoliating and stimulating new skin growth. Now that we have a clean face, let's start steaming. The luxe approach is to use a facial steamer. While not excessively pricey, they DO take up space. Depending on your storage capabilities, you may choose to forego getting one. You say that you do not have a facial steamer? No problem! I'm sure you have a big pot and a towel. Fill up a big pot with water and heat until the water is close to boiling. Find a comfy location to place the pot (or pour the water into a glass bowl), lean over, and cover your head and face area with a towel to trap the steam.

Close your eyes, breathe slowly, and listen to your spa music. Set your timer for five minutes and let the magic begin! To make your steaming ritual extra special, you can add a few drops of essential oil to the water. Lavender is calming. Eucalyptus helps with nasal congestion. If your skin is irritated, try adding chamomile. Another treat is to use a eucalyptus washcloth afterwards. Place a washcloth in a bowl of cold water with a few drops of eucalyptus essential oil. Roll up the washcloth, place it in a zip-lock bag, and refrigerate. You might want to prepare several, as you will be in heaven using these after steaming or a workout!

After steaming, rinse your face or use your exquisite eucalyptus washcloth. Now, you can decide on a face mask. Oh, the choices you have! Do you want something soothing, tightening, pore-minimizing, relaxing, or nourishing? There are different ways of "masking" as well. I started out years ago with peel-off face masks. These help to refine your pores and have some exfoliating properties. Charcoal masks are great for detoxifying but can be a bit drying. Cream masks are great for dry skin. If you have sensitive skin or want a cooling, soothing sensation then gel masks are for you. There are even thermal masks that heat up. These can be refreshing, and the heat opens pores. Sheet masks have become very popular. These "sheets" look like masks with cutouts for your eyes, nostrils, and mouth. They are infused with ingredients, and you can find a sheet mask to accomplish whatever you want to achieve.

Apply your chosen face mask, put two cucumber slices over your eyes, and RELAX for the duration of the mask. Ahh, this feels good! Remove the mask, use your toner, apply your favorite serum and moisturizer, and then get ready to create lovely locks, nails, and toes. Or call it a day and enjoy being your beautiful self!

## What Does a Skin Toner Do?

You might have thought, "Should I use a toner after washing my face? What does it do?" Those were questions I had until I started using a toner. Now mind you, I only started using one because I got BOTTLES of it as a free gift when I bought some face cream and perfume. I decided to try it since I had so much and boy, was I surprised.

Toners today are multi-taskers! A toner removes the debris and dirt that is left over after washing your face. I was AMAZED at how much dirt was left on my face after washing it, even if I used a face brush to clean it. Not so much of an a-ha moment as a "Yuck" moment. Other benefits include stabilizing the pH of your face, shrinking pores (yes, please), temporarily tightening the face, and creating a perfect canvas for serums and moisturizers to be applied. They are also refreshing and can moisturize. Sounds good!

You might be wondering what type of toner you need. There are various toner options and price points. A very basic, been-around-

FOREVER option is witch hazel. You can get it in any drugstore and it is inexpensive. The drawback is that it includes alcohol which can have a drying effect. This might be okay if you have skin that is on the oily side. Exfoliating toners include AHAs/BHAs/PHAs as ingredients and can be a real help for girls with combination skin or skin that is oily or prone to blemishes.

Girls who need more hydration and moisture should look for different ingredients. Nourishing toners have ingredients that include hyaluronic acid, aloe vera, rosewater, and cucumber. All the major makeup brands have a toner. Some may focus on clarifying; others brighten or moisturize. Select one that has the "special features" you are interested in or stick with the basics. So, is a toner worth it? I say YES. I want my face as clean as possible before I start with my other lotions and potions to keep my skin looking and feeling great!

## What Is the Difference Between a Serum and a Moisturizer?

What is the difference between a serum and a moisturizer, and do I need both? Serums are lightweight and filled with active ingredients that penetrate your skin. They are designed to target a specific skin-care issue, such as anti-aging or dryness, and can penetrate up to 10 layers! A moisturizer is thicker and focuses on hydrating your skin. It may include other ingredients such as retinol or SPF. Most girls can benefit from using both!

Serum can be used in the morning, at night, or both. You want to apply a serum after cleansing your face. You'll only need a few drops as serums are concentrated and a little goes a long way. If you use one containing hyaluronic acid, you'll see an improvement in your skin tone and hydration. Other serums can fight free radicals. These have active ingredients such as vitamins C and E. Not only do they help to protect your skin, but they can also stimulate collagen production!

Vitamin C can also help to brighten your complexion, reduce dark spots, and even out your skin tone by exfoliating and improving cell turnover.

If you have sensitive skin or are prone to acne or rosacea, serums with green tea, chamomile, or aloe vera can be refreshing and calming to your skin. The anti-inflammatory properties can help get rid of the redness. If you want to improve your texture, then a serum with retinol or glycolic acid is the one for you! They help with cell turnover and collagen building, and you may see fine lines and wrinkles disappear! So, before you invest in a serum, think about what you want it to do. A girl with sensitive skin doesn't need the added irritation of retinol. If you have oily skin, a serum may be all you need.

Moisturizers hydrate the skin. They are heavier than a serum and do not penetrate as deep but are hard workers too! If you are going to use both, apply the moisturizer after the serum. When your skin is hydrated, it is protected from the environment and can reduce inflammation. Moisturizers can also make blemishes less noticeable. Skin that is moisturized is less dry and develops wrinkles at a slower rate. Moisturizers may contain some of the same special ingredients as serums, so you'll be getting double duty.

They come in various versions: creams, lotions, and ointments. Lotions are lightweight and water-based, which means you won't be left with a thick, greasy feeling. Creams are thicker and do a fantastic job of hydrating the skin. Ointment is heavy-duty and is made with oils. If you are going to use one, it is better to use it at night. I ALWAYS use a moisturizer during the day with an SPF of 30 or higher.

Sometimes, I may use BB cream to save time. BB stands for beauty balm or blemish balm. It is a lightweight foundation and moisturizer in one. It provides light coverage, SPF protection and moisturizes my skin. There are also CC creams that help with color correcting. If you have dark spots, redness, or sallow skin these may be a better choice.

You say you want it all? Well, there are DD creams that are being created. These are "dynamic do-all" or daily defense creams.

If you aren't sure if you need both serum and a moisturizer, start with a serum and see if it does the trick. If you need both and are on a budget, consider a serum and a BB or CC cream. While a BB or CC cream doesn't provide the full coverage of a foundation, they are budget-friendly and can be used instead of a moisturizer and foundation. Some girls use moisturizer in the morning and a serum at night.

There are all different price points as well. Pricier doesn't necessarily mean better. I love that serums penetrate so well but I also need to hydrate, hydrate, hydrate! Look for sales at the drugstore or when beauty products go on sale at the cosmetic counter. I find that Macy's routinely has 15% off beauty products. A great way to try new skin products is to get a "gift with purchase" where you get a variety of products in smaller sizes that you can test and see if they work for you.

## Be Like a Snake and Exfoliate

Exfoliation has so many benefits that if you aren't doing it, you'll want to start! Just like reptiles shed their old, dead skin, we need to do so too. Exfoliation is a process that helps shed or remove dead, dry skin so your skin can glow and look more youthful. The process can improve circulation and stimulate collagen. When you get rid of dead skin cells, serums and moisturizers can penetrate more easily and work better.

Another benefit is that your pores are unclogged, which can help reduce acne breakouts. You may notice a more even skin tone as well. Hmm, can it reduce fine lines and wrinkles? Well, yes, by stimulating collagen, renewing your cells, and making it easier for your lotions and potions to penetrate, it certainly can reduce fine lines and wrinkles!

Sounds good, so now you are wondering how to exfoliate? There are a lot of ways to exfoliate. You can utilize a facial wash or scrub. These are a bit grainy or feel like they have sand particles in them. A facial cleansing brush or facial loofah provides a bit more strength. Exfoliation does not have to be done every day, shoot for three times a week.

Another choice can be Retin A products. These come in various strengths. Start low and go slow. You need to ease into using Retin A, otherwise you might actually look like a snake with your skin peeling. I made the mistake once of overdoing Retin A and for days people told me I had crumbs on my face. Although, it wasn't crumbs, it was the dead skin cells peeling off my face! Not a good look and it was quite embarrassing. Remember to start low and go slow!

The strongest exfoliating power comes from chemical peels and can be done at home, by a dermatologist, or aesthetician. Chemical peels can be harsh and can damage your skin if not done skillfully, so a professional is recommended if you go this route. Keep in mind you may need a few days to recover from a chemical peel. Your face may be quite red or blistery afterwards so plan accordingly!

And don't just exfoliate your face. Your neck and decolletage need it too. Have you ever seen that woman with breathtaking gorgeous skin who forgot about her neck and decolletage? It is almost a living "before and after" photo and we only want to be showing the world the "after" results! Even your body can benefit from exfoliation with a body brush. Yes, it can feel funny "brushing" your body before taking a bath or shower, but the after-effects will be silky, soft skin.

## Needles Aren't Just for Sewing Anymore!

Needles can play an important role in having beautiful skin. While no one wants to feel like a pincushion, micro-needling, and facial acupuncture can produce natural results that last! So, what is micro-needling? It is a roller with many needles attached to it that is used on the face. Yikes, does it hurt? Not really, the practitioner applies a numbing solution after cleansing your face. The idea is to produce a LOT of little "micro-traumas" that will stimulate blood flow and collagen development. You may want to hide out afterwards (makeup is discouraged for a day or two afterwards). Micro-needling can produce fast results and is good for people suffering from acne, scars, fine lines, and dull skin tone.

Cosmetic facial acupuncture is very similar to micro-needling but takes it a step further. The Mei Zen method not only treats the face but seeks to improve the energy within the entire body. In fact, Mei Zen translates to "beautiful person" and the goal is to be beautiful inside and out! Facial acupuncture needles go deeper than micro-needling.

The procedure increases blood circulation and promotes the development of elastin and collagen. It reduces inflammation, lifts, firms, and tightens! And you'll see less facial puffiness. The face reshapes itself to your natural, youthful state. For women who want to avoid fillers or Botox, facial acupuncture can produce the results they want without putting synthetic or toxic substances in the body. You end up with a more beautiful YOU without a frozen face or the risk of fillers giving you a bizarre look.

Keep in mind that you can't wave a magic wand, or magic needle, and erase years of damage. While you'll see improvement, micro-needling and facial acupuncture won't make you look decades younger. The good news is that if these procedures are started when you notice signs of aging, you can significantly delay wrinkles, saggy skin, and a dull complexion.

Facial acupuncture, also known as facial rejuvenation, is not a "one-and-done" procedure. It requires frequent (1–2/week) initial treatments and then you can go into the "maintenance" mode with a treatment every 4–6 weeks. I started facial acupuncture years ago on a cruise. It was part of a spa package option. Little did I know that the three treatments were a start and not an end! But boy has it been a good experience. Not only have I been able to maintain a tight, minimally wrinkled face, but it also gives me time to meditate during the treatment.

As a multi-tasker being able to beautify and meditate at the same time is a win-win! These are considerations when deciding if it is a good choice for you. If you do not have the time or have a real fear of needles, then the filler or Botox route might be for you. Keep in mind that "less is more" and be sure to pick a board-certified practitioner. You don't want to end up as a patient on the show "Botched" or look like a clown!

## Coconut Oil Isn't Just for Cooking!

You might be using coconut oil to fry your eggs or in your keto-friendly fat bomb, coffee creamer. What else can this heart-healthy oil do? Skin LOVES coconut oil. It is absorbed quickly, is an antioxidant, and has antifungal and antibacterial qualities. Use it as a lip moisturizer or gloss. Swap out your hand and body lotions for coconut oil. Finally, no more dry skin or hands!

It also makes an excellent eye and face moisturizer. Who knew? You say you can't give up your favorite face cream, try using coconut oil as a face pre-wash. Do you struggle to get that waterproof mascara off your lashes? Coconut oil can be used to remove makeup, even that stubborn waterproof mascara! Have you ever been ready to shave your legs and are out of shaving cream? Usually, this is discovered as you are in the shower and notice that you REALLY need to shave your legs or underarms. Oh no. Grab the coconut oil for a perfect shave.

Is your hair a bit lackluster? Coconut oil to the rescue! Did you know it can penetrate the hair shaft? Sleep with it on your hair overnight or if you have limited time, then 30–60 minutes with a shower cap will give you shiny hair. Did you wake up and the weather is not cooperating and giving you frizzy hair? On dry hair, a little coconut oil can ease the frizz and give you dramatic shine.

Would you like to relax? Coconut oil makes a fantastic massage oil. It melts quickly, is smooth, and smells like a tropical breeze. Give yourself a foot massage or have your honey massage your back. If things progress, coconut oil is also known as a great natural lubricant.

## I'll Take a Vowel Vanna

Remember as a child repeating over and over "A, E, I, O, U" to learn the vowels? Well, it turns out that repeating the vowels is good for your face too! Yes, repeating in an exaggerated manner "A, E, I, O, U" helps to exercise your facial muscles and tighten them. This can lead to plumper lips and a more toned jawline. And the best part is that you can do it ANYWHERE.

I especially like to "say my vowels" in the car while I am driving. I am sure passengers in other cars might think, "What is that lady doing?", but it is an easy way to get it done. Or you could do it while watching Wheel of Fortune. Strive for five minutes a day. To "up the ante" you can also tone your face with a pink silicone device that looks like those plastic lips you played with as a kid. You might find them under "Lip Trainer" or "Face Slimmer" when you search Google. You use the device along with saying your vowels for extra resistance. It is a crazy look, so this one should be done at home.

Now you may be wondering if you start a facial exercise regimen, will it really plump up your cheeks, reduce jowls, and improve your neckline? Yes, it can! JAMA Dermatology 2018 did a study of middle-aged women. They completed thirty-two facial exercises over twenty weeks and appeared almost three years younger! The downside is that it can be time-consuming. For the first two months, they exercised their face every day for thirty minutes, then dropped to 3–4 times a week for another three months.

There is anecdotal information that women who do facial exercises, sometimes called facial yoga, at an earlier age show very few wrinkles or sagging skin when they get to middle age. So, the earlier you can start the better! There are other "target" exercises that you might want to try for specific areas. Do you remember making "fish faces" at your brother or sister? Who knew that "Fish Face" exercises your cheeks? Pucker up while sucking in your cheeks then try to smile (It's hard not to smile while doing it) for about ten seconds. Puffy Face is the opposite; puff out your cheeks with air then try to move the air from cheek to cheek and hold it for five seconds in each cheek.

Classic facial exercises include the Neck Curl Up, Chin Up, and Tongue Twister. Neck Curl Up sounds like an ab curl-up and is kind of similar. You lay on your back, put your tongue to the roof of your mouth, and move your chin to your chest. You only need to lift 2–3 inches off the ground for it to be effective and boy, does this one work the neck muscles! Chin Up helps the lower part of your face and jawline. With your mouth closed, push your jaw forward, then lift your bottom lip up and out, and hold for ten seconds. The Tongue Twister also targets the lower part of your face and your chin. This one is fun. Put your tongue on the roof of your mouth in the back and hum! The tongue provides pressure and humming creates vibration getting your muscles activated.

A super simple exercise to lift your face and jaw is to make a wide smile with your mouth closed and hold it for ten seconds. For the ambitious, you can repeat the smile while showing a little of your teeth for ten seconds, then more of your teeth for ten seconds, and then finish looking like the Big Bad Wolf exposing all teeth (no gums) for ten seconds. Do you have friends that give you air kisses? Maybe they are really getting some lip exercises in! The Air Kisses routine involves giving four air kisses then putting two fingers on your lips and blowing another four air kisses. Another easy exercise is Surprise Me, which focuses on your forehead muscles. It could also be called "frighten me" as you make your eyes wide without crinkling your forehead. Look "surprised" or "frightened" for ten seconds.

All these exercises are meant to be repeated at least once. Remember to start slow and take your time building up. While we are aiming to stay beautiful or reverse the hands of time, you do not want to look like you are in pain from overexercising your facial muscles! With so many choices to exercise your face, there is no reason not to test out a few!

## How To Look Five Years Younger Fast!

An overlooked trick to almost instantly looking younger is whitening your teeth. Really? Yes, really. Our teeth yellow as we age, and whiter teeth connote youthfulness. I watched a makeover show years ago. You know, the type of show where they take a 40- or 50-year-old who is a little frumpy, slightly overweight, has a bad haircut and they do their magic, and everyone goes "Wow." Well, the very first thing the miracle workers did was whiten the teeth of each contestant. The hosts were not wrong. A study done by Oral B, the toothbrush people, concluded that by whitening teeth, a person was perceived on average to be 20% more attractive and five years younger. Sign me up!

Now, you are asking what is the fastest way to whiten your teeth? There are toothpastes and strips you can get at any drugstore. These will help to lighten teeth a few shades, but if you need to jump-start a blinding smile, then you need to go the professional route. Yes, it can be pricey, but it is worth it. Save up if you must do so and treat yourself.

The benefits are that your teeth will be whitened by several levels, and you'll have mouth trays that are perfectly matched to your teeth that you can use for maintenance. Most dentists will want you to buy the maintenance tooth whitening gel from them. I did the first time, then did my research, and found it online for half the price! I have used the mouth trays and gotten the same whitening gel the dentist has used for years. I get a lot of compliments on my smile and white teeth.

If you have extensive yellowing, the professional whitening will only be able to do so much. Veneers may be a consideration if the whitening is not going to accomplish your goals. Just be careful not to go too white. The whitest color may look fabulous on the color grid, but in real life, it may scream "fake."

Okay, so you've gotten your teeth to their optimal pearl color, look five years younger, and want to maintain the look! The "go-to" plan should consist of using a gentle tooth whitening toothpaste (with fluoride), preferably with an electric or sonic toothbrush. Flossing is a must to keep your gums healthy and remove offending food. Test out different types of floss until you find one you like and then use it at least once a day. There are even water-based flossers that feel wonderful, and you'll be amazed at how they massage your gums and remove hidden bits of food from between your teeth.

Continue periodically with your at-home whitening using your mouth trays. Keep your routine dental appointments where you get a professional cleaning. After all this work, you don't want to get cavities or gum disease! A professional cleaning and polishing every six months helps remove minor stains and keep your teeth looking good.

And you'll want to avoid or at least minimize the effects of tooth-staining food and beverages. No, you don't have to give up coffee, red wine, or blueberries. Tips to prevent staining include drinking water between sips of coffee or wine. Using a straw is another option but may look silly if you are drinking coffee or red wine. A major offender is sports drinks, especially if they contain vitamins. I had been using an after-work-out drink and the very bottom of my teeth started turning a yellowish-orange color. My hygienist noticed it and told me to stop the sports drink or at least use a straw. It took a while to remove the stains, and I now take my vitamins in pill form!

Brushing your teeth shortly after eating an offending food can help. A toothbrush and paste are not handy? Consider eating an apple to help cleanse your teeth or hard cheese can neutralize acids that can stain teeth. Who knew? I guess the French got it right by having a cheese course after the main meal.

## Does Red Light Therapy Get the Green Light?

Red light therapy can help with anti-aging by promoting collagen, strengthening connective tissue, and reducing fine lines. It has anti-inflammatory benefits and can also help clear up acne and make scars less noticeable. Great, but you wonder how you can get red light? You can go to a professional or do it yourself at home!

Dermatologists, aestheticians, and even some spas offer red light therapy. The professionals have red light therapy at a higher wavelength than the home-use models. The home red light machines have very tiny LED lights that provide red wave light when turned on. You place the machine very close to your face. Some devices have panels and others are masks. Think Freddie Kruger or Silence of the Lambs scary-style masks, although the intent is to cover your face and, in some cases, even your neck for an even distribution of the red light. For the DIY girl, you can find many different models available on the web.

Red light therapy does take some commitment as you'll need to devote about fifteen minutes a day several times a week if you are using it at home. Read the manufacturer's instructions for details on the specific machine if you go the DIY route as well as online reviews. There are also different "strengths." Higher nanometers, such as 630 nm are more effective than lower levels. Prices can vary widely with basic models starting at around $350 and the high-tech masks can be $3,000 or more.

Some of the mask devices have a strap that allows it to stay in place and you can be mobile. They are a bit bulky, but you could easily do a household chore or watch TV. I found it difficult to do tasks requiring fine motor detail such as painting my nails or writing. I have used panels and a mask.

The advantage of panels is that you can use them on other parts of your body. There are claims that red light therapy can help to minimize the appearance of cellulite and is beneficial for wound healing. The panels can easily be adjusted to other areas of your body whereas the mask would be difficult to place on another body area. The disadvantage of panels is that you cannot move around like you can when using a mask that straps on. Whether you seek professional treatment or get your red-light treatment at home, red light therapy definitely gets the green light!

And it's not only what we do to the outside that counts, but also how we care for ourselves on the inside. Let's learn about how our nutrition choices impact how our skin looks and the benefits to our internal workings!

# NUTRITION

# Vitamin D Gets an A+!

I was shocked years ago when I was told that I had a severe vitamin D deficiency. I drank a few cups of milk a day, lived in sunny Los Angeles, and either hiked or walked my dog daily. What happened? Vitamin D is produced when we are exposed to UVB rays.

Looking back on it, I used UVA/UVB high SPF sunscreen along with wearing a hat. I wasn't sure why my consumption of milk wasn't enough, but I was placed on prescription-strength vitamin D for six weeks. So, what's the big deal about vitamin D? Vitamin D helps your body absorb calcium which keeps our bones strong. No one wants osteoporosis! It also provides immune support and benefits the nervous system.

Do you know of a little old lady who fell and broke a hip due to osteoporosis? This is a condition that can be prevented. Most practitioners check vitamin D levels with an annual preventive exam and recommend bone analysis as women get older. If there is a deficit or they note weakening of the bones, there are interventions that can be initiated to strengthen the bones.

Vitamin D enhances the absorption of calcium. Do you take a calcium supplement? Check out the label – it probably contains Vitamin D too! What else can it do? Vitamin D helps to prevent falls by improving muscle tone, and strong muscles improve our balance. Would you like to prevent cognitive decline? Yes, who wouldn't?! One study showed that the risk of dementia was 54% higher in people who had low vitamin D levels. Several studies concluded that people with normal Vitamin D levels have a reduced risk of early death. Goodbye, Grim Reaper!

The key to preventing a cold may not be orange juice but rather vitamin D! It reduces inflammation and strengthens the immune system. When we turn the clocks back and it is cold outside, everyone gets less sunshine. No wonder we get those pesky wintertime colds. Children and adults with low levels are more likely to get a cold or respiratory infection.

Vitamin D is also linked to reducing the incidence of auto-immune disorders by 22%. Type 2 diabetes is at epidemic rates. Could vitamin D help? Yes! Vitamin D has been shown to reduce inflammation, insulin resistance and preserve beta cell function. It may also have some benefits in reducing cancer risk by preventing or slowing tumor growth.

Okay, you say you're sold. Load me up with vitamin D! While we want to have an adequate level of vitamin D, this is one vitamin where more is not better. Too much vitamin D can cause problems such as cardiac arrhythmias and kidney stones. It is a fat-soluble vitamin which means it is absorbed into your fat and stays in our bodies longer. (Water-soluble vitamins are easily flushed out of our system.)

The best way to know if you are already getting enough vitamin D is through a lab test. If you need to supplement there are choices: a capsule, sunshine, or vitamin D-rich food. There are not a lot of foods that are naturally rich in vitamin D, but several are fortified, meaning that vitamin D has been added. These include cereals, bread, orange juice, and milk. Foods that are rich in vitamin D include fish, such as salmon, tuna, swordfish, and sardines.

Fifteen minutes of sunshine helps our body make vitamin D and with this natural approach your body won't overproduce vitamin D. Your body knows when you've gotten enough! If you choose a capsule, you might be confused between D2 and D3. D2 comes from plants and is used in fortified foods. D3 is what your body produces and is in animal products. Both work, although D3 does a better job of raising vitamin D levels and sustains it longer. Wherever you get your vitamin D, go for it! This is one vitamin that definitely gets an A+ in my book.

# Whey Protein or Plant Protein – What's the Difference?

You've decided you want to add a protein drink to help build your muscles or provide extra protein as a nutritional supplement. Great! There are several choices out there with the main differences between protein powders being either a whey or plant-based protein. What is whey? When cheese is being produced, the liquid that separates from the milk is called whey. It is full of protein and amino acids. Plant protein powders are usually derived from soy, pea, or rice protein. So how do you choose between them? If you are lactose intolerant or want a vegan-friendly choice, then the plant-based powder is your go-to! Both help to build muscle and can support your weight loss or maintenance goals.

Whey protein is a complete protein, is chock full of nutrition, has all nine amino acids, and is easily digestible. Remember Little Miss Muffet? She sat on her tuffet eating curds and whey. She was one smart girl! Amino acids help to build muscle and whey protein includes leucine which rapidly promotes muscle growth. Bring on those toned arms and abs! One benefit of dairy products, particularly whey protein, is a reduction in blood pressure for people who have hypertension. Whey protein has ACE inhibitors which relax blood vessels. You may be able to reduce or prevent the use of blood pressure medications if you incorporate whey protein into your diet.

Whey protein can help people who have type 2 diabetes. It helps to modulate blood sugar and can be a good addition to a diabetes disease management plan. Wow, what else does whey protein do? It can reduce inflammation, promote antioxidants, and help to control overall and bad cholesterol.

Protein is filling and satisfies you when you are hungry. Instead of grabbing a candy bar, sip on a satisfying whey protein drink! (Be sure to select one with a low sugar content.) A scoop of powder usually has about 20–25 grams of protein. It is nutritious and will keep you satisfied for hours!

Most plant proteins are not a complete protein, meaning they do not have all nine amino acids, but still provide a lot of benefits and are nutrient-dense. Combining different plant proteins may result in getting all nine amino acids. Do you need to increase fiber in your diet? Plant proteins are here to help you! The increased fiber helps you develop good gut bacteria.

Fiber helps to regulate blood sugar and keeps you feeling full. One study showed that consuming 35% or more of your protein from plants reduced HbA1c levels. The positive effect on blood sugar can be an added benefit for those with type 2 diabetes. Another study saw a reduction in mortality for people between 50–71 years old by switching out just 3% of their animal protein intake to plant protein. Hmm, could plant protein be the fountain of youth?

Plant proteins include phytochemicals that contribute to a healthier you! They help build muscle and improve immunity. Are you concerned about the environment? Since plant proteins do not come from animals, you may feel they are more environmentally friendly.

Fabulous, now you asking yourself how much protein do I need? As a guide, you can multiply your weight by 0.36 to determine how much protein you need daily. For example, a 120-lb woman would need 43.2 grams of protein a day (120 x 0.36 = 43.2). Keep in mind this is protein from all sources.

Great sources of complete protein include meat, edamame, tofu, eggs, tuna, cottage cheese, turkey, quinoa, salmon, parmesan cheese, and Greek yogurt. For example, one cup of Greek yogurt has 20 grams of protein. Grabbing a piece of parmesan cheese? One ounce has 11 grams of protein. A serving of salmon packs 35 grams of protein. Turkey isn't just for Thanksgiving. A 4-ounce serving has 25 grams. Debating between a burger and a can of tuna for lunch? A can of tuna is low in calories and fat and will give you an impressive 33 grams of protein! Instead of ice cream or cookies, I like having a cup of cottage cheese. Not only is it yummy, but you also get 25 grams of protein too.

You may want to supplement your diet with a protein powder if you are not getting enough protein in your diet. Whey protein powders tend to have a milder taste and blend well whereas plant protein powders can be on the earthy side and may clump a bit more. Pay attention to added sugar and avoid it as much as possible. Try different protein drinks. You may want to mix it up with a vanilla pea protein drink one day and a creamy double-chocolate whey protein another day. The important thing is to get enough protein to stay lean, toned, and fabulous!

## Should I Try Intermittent Fasting?

You've heard of it, but aren't quite sure what is intermittent fasting? It is time-restricted eating where you consume zero calories (water, tea, coffee, etc. are allowed) for a set time period and eat only during the non-fasting period. The fasting period can vary. A popular schedule is to fast sixteen hours a day and eat during an eight-hour window. Most people skip breakfast and eat lunch and dinner. Lunch could be at 11:30 am and you would stop eating by 7:30 pm. Sounds doable, doesn't it?

Another way to fast is the "alternating days" method. You eat anytime you want one day, then the next day fast or consume a very small meal of about 500 calories. Although for me, I would probably eat a LOT more calories on my regular day and not reap as many benefits. Another method is called "5:2." You eat normally for five days a week and then fast for two days. It may work for you, but this would be my least favorite method.

So why would you want to try intermittent fasting? Intermittent fasting provides a wide variety of health benefits. It helps people lose weight.

When you are limiting when you eat, your body goes into a state of ketosis which helps to burn fat. There are many other benefits too.

These include increasing the anti-aging human growth hormone, reducing insulin resistance, increasing your metabolic rate, preserving muscle mass, melting belly fat, reducing inflammation, increasing a brain hormone that is associated with nerve cell regeneration, and extending life span (at least in mice). Wow, why isn't EVERYONE doing it? Lifestyle and habits can be hard to change.

If you like a lot of cream or sugar in your morning coffee or tea, it can be tough to go without. It can be hard not to grab a drink without calories or not eat anything until almost noon. Do you like a late-night snack or popcorn while watching a movie on Netflix or a glass of wine before bed? Well, that is out unless you delay your eight-hour window well into the afternoon. However, understanding the MANY health benefits can motivate you. As with all diets or major lifestyle changes, it is a good idea to discuss it with your health practitioner. Intermittent fasting may not be a good choice for pregnant or lactating women, people with diabetes or other health conditions.

No one can just jump into intermittent fasting without an adjustment period. There can be side effects during the first month while you get used to your new eating pattern. You may feel hungry, tired, have headaches, feel nauseated, and sleep poorly. I WELCOMED dreams where I was eating my favorite foods! I admit it, I was a cranky girl for a while.

It is easier if you ease into intermittent fasting. If you normally eat from 7 am to 9 pm, then start narrowing your window to twelve hours of non-fasting for a week or two, then ten hours and, eventually, get down to eight hours. Water is your friend. As you start drinking more water you will be better hydrated, which offers its own health benefits. I find that drinking alkaline water helps to reduce my appetite. Many people swear by sparkling water to control their hunger pangs!

You might want to focus on the types of food you eat as well. A keto-friendly approach pairs well with intermittent fasting. Try to avoid simple carbohydrates, white flour, refined foods, and sugar. Yikes, you say you LOVE bread and candy. What do you do? There is keto bread available, and it is low-calorie; 40 calories a slice! I find it tastes better if toasted or used with a sandwich I'll heat in the microwave.

A Mediterranean-style diet is also a good choice. Lots of protein, vegetables, whole grains, and healthy fats such as olive oil. If you are a chocoholic, try switching to a keto-friendly chocolate bar or a dark chocolate bar with a high percentage of cocoa. Chocolate protein powders can curb your cravings and is a nice reward after exercising. Everyone will have times when their schedule doesn't work well with life. When you are on vacation or have houseguests, it can seem rude or antisocial to stick to a strict schedule. Or you are going out with the girls and don't feel like drinking sparkling water all night.

Even if you can't keep to your intermittent fasting schedule EVERY day, it's okay. You can get back on your schedule. Intermittent fasting is a marathon, not a sprint and it is a lifestyle choice that works for so many people. Think about if it might be right for you!

## Fabulous, Fat-Free Water!

The benefits of being properly hydrated are many! Water helps keep your joints properly lubricated, reducing joint pain. Did you know that the cartilage in your joints is 80% water? (Maybe you CAN do that exercise class this afternoon!) When you are hydrated, your brain functions better. Dehydration can make you feel tired and cranky and reduce brain function.

The National Council on Aging states that even as little as a 2% fluid loss can impact your memory, mood, and response time. Most people who reach for candy or coffee in the afternoon when they are feeling a bit dragged out are actually dehydrated. Forget the Snickers bar and reach for a glass or two of water! Water helps with breaking down fibrous foods and keeps everything moving smoothly through you.

What else can water do? Upping your water intake by even 1% (Yes, you can do this!) can keep you feeling full and reduce your intake of sugar, fat, and cholesterol-laden food. Hmm, maybe you can drop those few pounds you've been meaning to lose. Staying hydrated helps with maintaining your temperature, keeps your heart working better, plumps up your skin, and reduces headaches and your chances of getting a kidney stone. Who knew that water had so MANY anti-aging properties?!

You say you understand, but you don't like drinking water. You can overcome this and get those six to eight glasses a day. One formula to determine your water needs is taking your weight, dividing it by 3, and then drinking that number of ounces. If you weigh 120 lb, divide by 3 to get 40 and add "ounces." A woman weighing 120 lb would need a minimum of 40 ounces of water a day. Of course, if it is very hot outside or you are exercising you may need to up your intake.

So how do you take in that much water when you'd rather have a diet Coke? You can try mineral water or alkaline water. These have different tastes and are smoother. I also find that alkaline water seems to decrease my appetite. A perfect choice for the afternoon or early morning. Sparkling water with lemon or lime can be a special drink. You could also add a few berries to make it pretty and then you have a little treat after you drink your water.

Try drinking eight ounces as soon as you wake up before you grab that coffee or tea. I keep a glass of water next to my bed and drink it as soon as I get out of bed. It is healthy and an easy way to get some ounces in. Some girls like using a water bottle that has the ounces listed and take sips throughout the day. Drinking eight ounces or even six ounces before meals can reduce the number of calories you eat at a meal and is another easy way to up your water intake.

Test out different temperatures. Ice cold, room temperature, or even hot water are options. I like ice-cold water after coming in from hot weather or after exercising. Room-temperature water is easier to gulp down while working or before meals. Hot water in a coffee mug or teacup with lemon can be very refreshing, especially if you are trying to reduce your caffeine intake. It sounds "Ew" until you try it and believe me, it can become addictive!

There are also water flavorings available that increase the palatability of drinking water. Or create your own flavored water! Who doesn't LOVE cucumber or strawberry water at the spa? Yes, I'll take another glass! You can cut up cucumbers or other fruit and put slices in a pitcher to add flavor. Be sure you make enough, as other family members may get hooked too!

Once you start drinking water, in whatever form that suits you best, you will feel better, look better, and be a lot healthier! We spend so much time and money on lotions, potions, pick-me-up beverages, and the latest wonder diet when drinking pure, refreshing, and inexpensive water could replace so many of these. We've all heard about KISS; Keep It Simple Silly. Try keeping it simple with water and reap the myriad benefits of nature's liquid gold!

## Should I Be Drinking a Green Drink?

You see green drinks everywhere; in the grocery and convenience store refrigerated sections, on shelves in the nutrition aisle, heck, your friends may be carrying one around with them and drinking what looks like pond scum. What are they and should you be drinking one?

Some green drinks are a blend of juices and superfoods. Think kale, celery, spinach, cucumber, or lettuce mixed with citrus juice. Despite the green color, these green drinks tend to be very refreshing and tasty. They are great if you are not getting enough green, leafy veggies in your diet and want a quick, easy way to supplement your diet. Pay attention to the sugar content, as some drinks are high in sugar, which negates many of the health benefits.

Other green drinks, especially powders that are added to water, are a powerhouse of nutrients. They include the usual dark green, leafy veggies, but can also include vitamins, minerals, superfood blends, prebiotics, and probiotics. Wowza! You'll need to compare labels and prices. Keep in mind that the most nutrient-dense powders are pricier but can replace your array of multivitamins and other nutritional supplements. You might SAVE money and have better nutrition by taking in one of these green drinks a day.

I like nutrient-dense green drinks as they give me the vitamins, minerals, and other "goodies" my body needs. Since I mix it with twenty ounces of water, it keeps me hydrated! I also find that I lose the midday hunger and sugar cravings. Whether this is from being well hydrated, drinking an alkaline beverage, or getting better nutrition I cannot say. It might be from any or all of these, all I know is it works!

So, while all of this sounds GREAT, why do you not see everyone with a green drink? The first drawback is taste. Unless a LOT of sugar is added, the high-nutrient drinks can have a funky taste. Some can be quite bitter and unpleasant. Other green powders are an acquired taste that gets better with time and after you see results.

How you prepare it can improve the taste as well. Some people like it better with ice, others like it at room temperature, and others mix it into a smoothie. I have tried a LOT of green powder mixes. While some were very difficult to drink, others were pleasant. My all-around favorite is AG1. It is a super nutritious green powder drink with everything anyone could want in it. It dissolves well and the taste is palatable. While it can be a little more expensive than other mixes, when you compare everything that is packed into one tablespoon of this powder, you cannot find a better bargain in my book!

# Is Sugar Poison?

Did you know that Americans consume 300% more sugar than we should every year? To say we have a sweet tooth is an understatement. So, how much should we be taking in? The American Heart Association recommends that women have an intake of no more than 25 grams a day (men can have 36 grams a day). As a reference, one sugar packet contains four grams.

Excessive sugar consumption is associated with obesity and inflammation. In studies with rats, excess sugar consumption led to increases in opioid-type hormones. There are anecdotal reports of sugar addiction in humans. Who hasn't felt they were in seventh heaven after having a glorious piece of sugary cake or a hot fudge sundae? Yum!

You might have heard that too much sugar is poison. Oh no, say it isn't true! Some studies suggest that consuming a lot of sugar interferes with appetite-regulating hormones, ghrelin and leptin. This means if you eat too much sugar, it can prevent you from feeling full and you'll continue to graze all day.

Some people call refined sugar "the white death" because of the damage it can do to our bodies. Too much refined sugar is associated with interfering with a protein that can lead to heart muscle issues, age our cells, decrease muscle elasticity, and reduce the immune response. Yikes, anything else? Well, since you asked, yes, you have an increased risk for cardiovascular disease, diabetes, cognitive disorders, retina issues, high blood pressure, and cholesterol to name a few. And don't forget you can get cavities from too much sugar and where did those love handles come from?

Keep in mind that you don't have to give up ALL sugar. The biggest contributor to our sugar intake is sugary drinks. Look the next time you decide to get an Orange Crush or a sweet coffee from Starbucks. You might be WAY over the recommended daily sugar grams, and you didn't even know it! You might be thinking you are helping your diet by purchasing "low fat" foods, but many times these foods are LOADED with sugar. Read the labels. The full-fat counterpart may be a more satisfying and healthier choice!

Keep in mind we are talking about added sugar. The sugar in a piece of fruit or a glass of milk that occurs naturally is fine. What you want to avoid is candy, cake, bakery treats, ice cream, and sugary drinks. If you are a cereal eater, check the label! Some cereals have more added sugar than a candy bar!

If you are a sugar hound, giving it up can take some time. Suddenly giving up sugar can cause cravings, headaches, nausea, bloating, irritability, and fatigue. You can start by easing back. Change from a full candy bar to one half. Look for low-sugar candy and cookie substitutes such as Atkins products. They are tasty with very low carbohydrates and sugar.

If you love your soda, start switching out the orange soda for an orange-flavored sparkling drink. Do you love your cheesecake at night? Wean yourself off with a mini cheesecake bite or maybe a mini bagel with light cream cheese. If you are used to a sweet treat after dinner, try having a cappuccino. It takes some time to drink, is warm, and you may feel full and satisfied and not need the usual goodie.

Eventually, you won't miss the sugar. I experienced sugar "crashes" when I was eating a lot of sugary items. I would get tired and feel down a few hours after my "sugar high" ended. Now, I satisfy my sweet tooth with ripe strawberries and cottage cheese, delicious mandarin oranges, or a low-sugar chocolate or vanilla protein drink. What sounds good to you?

## Help, I'm Dieting and Hit a Weight-Loss Plateau!

Nothing is more frustrating than changing your lifestyle and diet to be healthier and not seeing the results you were anticipating. You've given up cookies, cake, wine, and greasy French fries. You're getting your 10,000 steps a day in and saw some progress but now you are stuck! The scale isn't moving. You're even wondering if the scale is broken and recheck it holding your cat. No, the scale is working. What isn't working is your new plan. What is a girl to do?

It's important to realize that most girls will experience a weight-loss plateau as we are going through our weight-loss journey. Okay, well maybe not if you are trying to lose the five pounds you gained on vacation or over the holidays, but anyone who is trying to lose 10, 20, or 50 pounds that they've been carrying around will most likely encounter this common and very frustrating experience.

You've hit a plateau because your body is adjusting. You're feeding it less food and/or expending more energy and while you might lose the pounds quickly initially, your body then says, "Whoa, let's slow down here!" to put you into survival mode. It doesn't know that you WANT to shed weight. Your body is trying to protect you. It is "re-setting."

Have you heard of a set-point? It is the natural weight that your body wants to be. Now, if you've been twenty pounds overweight for a while, that weight is your set-point. You'll notice you'll stay within that range of plus or minus five pounds most of the time. When you begin to lose weight, you'll reach a new set-point that your body wants to maintain.

Plateaus can last 8–12 weeks. What? Yes, it can take that long for your new set-point to be established before your body stops fighting against you and will let you lose more weight. It doesn't mean you should give up! You can celebrate the weight loss you've achieved and maintain your healthy habits. If you haven't introduced weight-bearing exercise, this might be a good time to do so. Keep in mind that muscle weighs more than fat. So, part of the scale not moving might be related to developing more muscle than losing fat.

Ideally, you would have taken your measurements before starting your journey. I like to take a tape measure and track my calf, thigh, hip, waist, breast, and upper arm measurements as well as the percentage of fat. You can buy a fat analyzer, although there are a lot of smart scales that include it as a feature. I have a scale that gives me a TON of info: weight, fat percentage, water percentage, bone and muscle mass as well as the weather!

So, you understand this darn phenomenon of a plateau and have been powering through but want to jump-start the process a bit. There are tips to help nudge your body into getting back on the weight-loss track. Reducing your carbohydrate intake can help to burn calories. It is hard to maintain a very low carbohydrate nutrition plan but mixing it up can help.

Try increasing your protein intake and having some protein at every meal. You say you are not a big meat eater? Protein can also be found in fish, beans, tofu, quinoa, eggs, almonds, and even delicious protein drinks! Protein helps you feel full and satisfied and another bonus is that protein can boost your metabolic rate. Yes, please! If you haven't done so already, cut out the cocktails! While alcohol may be fun in a social setting or provide stress relief, it has zero nutritional value, adds a lot of empty calories, impedes your sleep, and reduces fat burning.

Everyone knows to eat more fiber. The benefits are that it helps you feel full, can decrease the calories you absorb from other food, and slow your digestion. So, bring on the apples and fiber cereal! Non-starchy veggies are great fiber sources too. A roasted tomato with a high-fiber piece of toast for breakfast? Sounds good! A salad or other greens with lunch and dinner? That's a can-do! A word of caution is that you should gradually increase your fiber. If you are going whole hog, be aware that increasing your fiber can also increase flatulence. You might want to invest in some Gas-X pills to avoid embarrassment when you are out and about. In addition to increasing fiber, get out that water bottle or splurge on sparkling water. Hydrate, hydrate, hydrate! I find that both alkaline water and sparkling water are refreshing and reduce my appetite.

Intermittent fasting can be another option. Limiting when you eat can preserve your basal metabolic rate and keep the fat burning, reduce your caloric intake, and maintain your muscle mass. The most effective versions include fasting between 16–48 hours. If not eating for two days doesn't sound too appealing, try the 16-hour version. Can you limit eating food between 10 am–6 pm or 12–8 pm? You can still have your coffee or tea in the morning and enjoy water all day.

If intermittent fasting isn't for you, consider tracking your food. A food diary will help you to really understand what you are taking in. Pay attention to portion sizes too. I joined a weight-loss food-delivery program once and my biggest "A-ha" was the portion sizes. They were TINY, yet they were the recommended portion sizes. We are so used to super-sized foods that you may not even realize the cereal you eat is five servings versus one. The grab-and-go bag of chips you bought might be 3 ½ servings versus 1. I use salad plates as my dinner plate and very small one-cup bowls to help keep me on track with portion control.

Other very important factors include getting 7–8 hours of sleep. If I don't sleep well, I am ravenous the next day. I keep trying to "wake up." My body feels out of whack and my appetite control hormones are sleepy too! Sleeping four hours a night can decrease your metabolic rate. Oh no, we don't need anything else to slow down our metabolism!

Keep your body moving. Even fidgeting can burn calories. Get up and move around every hour if you are sitting at a desk or on the couch watching TV or reading. If you've developed a regular exercise routine, that is great! Mix it up during the week. High Intensity Intermittent Training (HIIT) includes bursts of very strenuous exercise with periods of slower routines. It can be very effective. Try weight-bearing exercises and using weights (even light weights) to build muscle and no, you won't start to look like the Michelin man. Muscle burns fat even at rest! You can invest in some dumbbells and do a routine while watching TV. Five to fifteen minutes a day is doable and produces results.

Even if you are not losing weight, you may be losing inches. I was shocked when I lost some weight, and my pants were literally falling off my hips! It was a combination of resistance training and improved nutrition that reshaped my physique. So, try on some of your "fat clothes" and see if you are swimming in them. Some of those "when I lose 10lb" clothes might be fitting pretty well now. Try not to get stressed out about your stall. Spend time meditating to relax and visualize what you want to look like. Visualization is incredibly powerful as well as the power of positive thinking. You'll get where you want to be. Remember, it is a journey.

## Consequences of Cocktails at Eight

You've had a rough day or are ready to relax with friends and enjoy a beer, glass of wine, or a trendy cocktail. Time to relax and have some fun! Having a cocktail now and then is fine. Where we can get into trouble is if we are imbibing daily or to excess. So, what is excessive drinking? The CDC defines binge drinking as four or more drinks in a single session for women and five or more drinks for men. Keep in mind a "drink" is defined as 12 ounces of beer, 5 ounces of wine (not the 9-ounce version many bars and restaurants offer), or 1.5 ounces of 80-proof spirits.

The CDC defines "heavy drinking" as eight or more drinks a week for women and fifteen or more a week for men. The majority of binge and heavy drinkers are not alcohol-dependent or alcoholics. Not drinking or drinking moderately is recommended. Moderate drinking is defined as one drink for women and two for men. So, if you are used to having two glasses of wine (five-ounce version), two beers, or two cocktails nightly you are considered a heavy drinker.

Alcohol reduces our inhibitions and can lead to more risky behavior. Who hasn't become an outrageous flirt after having a few too many at least once? Or have you pigged out before bed because you became ravenously hungry and regretted ingesting all those calories the next morning? And speaking of sleeping, who has not experienced alcohol-fueled sleep disturbances? Yes, alcohol as a "nightcap" can help you to fall asleep, but it disrupts the REM cycle, and the quality of your sleep suffers. Even having less than one drink (think half a glass of wine or half a beer) for women reduced sleep quality by 9% and if you had a full drink, your sleep quality went down by 24%! Who wants to wake up feeling foggy, puffy, and with a headache? Not the best way to be a morning glory!

While everyone has probably had a hangover at one point, not everyone knows about the long-term consequences of overindulging with alcohol. Did you know that your risk of cancer increases with ongoing alcohol use? Yes, your risk of breast cancer or cancers of the gastrointestinal system are increased! Hmm, from just a few glasses of wine in the evening? Yes, alcohol produces a chemical called acetaldehyde that can damage your DNA. Damaged DNA can allow the bad cells to grow wildly and turn into tumors.

Overindulging can also lead to hypertension, heart disease, stroke, liver disease, and digestive disorders. Are you drinking more than what is recommended and are having indigestion? By cutting back, you might be able to ditch the Pepcid. People who drink alcohol consistently are also more prone to depression and anxiety. If you were having a few glasses of wine to relax and feel better, it can have the opposite effect! Other negative consequences include muscle wasting, demineralization of your bones, cognitive impairment, and respiratory issues. Becoming a shriveled and confused woman is NOT what anyone wants!

While you may be aware of the consequences, sometimes it is very difficult to break a habit. If you look forward to your evening libations, it can be hard to find a substitute. A glass of club soda might not do the trick. Tips to reduce your alcohol intake include changing your routine. Instead of going to a watering hole or sitting in front of the tube with a beer, go for a walk or the gym. Do something to get the endorphins going to feel happy and relaxed naturally!

Other tips include taking photos of yourself in a bathing suit before starting your no- or reduced-alcohol journey. Take another set of photos thirty days later and check out the changes! Did you lose a few pounds and look more toned, is your skin brighter, and are the puffy bags gone? You will start to feel GREAT in the morning from getting restful and rejuvenating sleep. Yes, you can do this!

The hardest part will be the first few weeks. If you normally get together with your friends for a girl chat with a bottle or two of wine, suggest going for a hike to talk and get some exercise. Instead of sitting in front of the TV wishing you had a beer, go to the movies where you'll be engaged and away from alcohol for a few hours. Look for alcohol substitutes. Some people do great with "near beer," virgin cocktails, or alcohol-free wine. I find that light cranberry juice is very satisfying. It is tangy, extremely refreshing, and pretty! You can even drink it out of a wine glass if you want.

Once you find a satisfying substitute, save it for when you would normally have a cocktail, so it becomes special and not something you'd drink throughout the day. If you find that you are having trouble not drinking and are concerned, there are multiple resources that can assist you. These include self-help books to guide you through the process, Alcoholics Anonymous, and a national 24-hour helpline (1-800-662-4357) that has information and other services available.

## Which Diet Plan Should I Choose?

So, you've decided to lose some weight or improve your nutrition. Good for you! We all know the foods to cut out: refined sugar, processed foods, seed oils, fast food, alcohol, etc. But you may wonder what diet plan you should use? There is DASH, the Mediterranean diet, flexitarian, WW, intermittent fasting, keto, and many others. You first need to think about what foods you like to eat. Are you a bread and pasta lover? Do you naturally crave veggies? Can you not go a day without a sweet? You'll want to pick a nutrition plan that will be a modification or improvement on your current eating habits and still allow you to eat your favorite foods. Instead of thinking "diet," which has a connotation of weight loss and deprivation, change your thinking to a nutrition plan, which will be a long-term plan to maintain a healthy lifestyle.

An overall winner and fan fave is the Mediterranean diet. This is a typical diet of people in Greece, Italy, and Spain. It consists mainly of plant-based foods such as fruits, vegetables, nuts, grains, healthy fat, and lean protein. It is veggie-heavy with limited amounts of lean protein such as fish or turkey. As with most people in Europe who enjoy life, small amounts of wine and dark chocolate are allowed and encouraged! It is a heart-healthy choice with numerous studies showing it helps with cardiovascular health, reducing type 2 diabetes, and controlling obesity.

Another popular plan is the Dietary Approaches to Stopping Hypertension or DASH diet. It has been around for a long time. If you've been diagnosed with pre-hypertension or hypertension, chances are you've been introduced, educated, and recommended to follow the DASH diet. It helps to control blood pressure and reduce bad cholesterol. Sodium, full-fat, and fatty meats are limited. The preferred foods are rich in magnesium, calcium, and potassium. These include fruits, vegetables, whole grains, low-fat dairy products, beans, nuts, fish, and poultry. There is a wide variety of food to choose from and it is easily adaptable to eating out. Both diets are highly recommended by the American Heart Association and are easy to maintain as a nutrition plan.

You've heard of a vegetarian diet but haven't heard of a flexitarian diet. What is it? It is basically a vegetarian diet that allows flexibility and the ability to eat meat on occasion. Most flexitarians eat somewhere between 9–28 ounces of meat a week. Think of two meatless days a week if you are at the upper end. You don't have to stick to a Beyond Burger if you are craving the real thing! The focus is on a plant-based diet, so most of your protein will come from plants (beans, edamame, tofu), plant-based milk products (almond or soy milk are examples), and of course, whole grains, veggies, and fruits.

You can see a theme here; vegetables, fruits, whole grains, and low-fat meats or limiting meat. Create your own nutrition plan if you don't want to strictly follow one of the established plans! Another good reference to help you change your eating habits is the series of books and a website called, "Eat This, Not That!". It gives great "better for you" options for foods that you may love, but are high in calories, fat, or lacking nutrition. The website is chock full of information, recipes, and "eat this, not that" choices when dining out at popular restaurants.

Are you more of a free spirit and don't want to be locked into a set list of foods? The points system with WW, also known as Weight Watchers, gives people a lot of choices and monitors their overall daily intake. No food is off-limits. Enjoy the birthday cake or grab a few Christmas cookies. The points system tracks your calories, fiber, protein, fats, and added sugar. This is a great option for bread and pasta lovers. It does require tracking of what you eat and there is a fee. Millions of people love the system and find that it works for them.

Intermittent fasting is another proven plan that has clinical studies showing that it has anti-aging properties and puts your body into ketogenic fat burning. This is a little more difficult plan to maintain, although, when people get used to it they really like it. It requires fasting and typically you don't take in any calories for at least 16 hours. There are a few different versions where you fast for fewer hours or eat five days a week and fast for two days. When you are not fasting, you can eat whatever you want. Of course, if you are making heart-healthy choices, you'll reap even better health benefits. People who practice intermittent fasting tend to be very well-hydrated as water, coffee, and tea are allowed during the fasting period and water consumption helps to control hunger pangs!

While intermittent fasting will put your body into a ketogenic fat-burning phase, it is not a keto diet. A keto diet is where you eat foods high in fat, protein and low in carbohydrates to put your body into ketogenesis. While it is fun to eat bacon, cheese, and steaks with abandon, it is a very restrictive diet where carbohydrates are extremely limited. I tried it once and found I was craving fruit. I did not find it to be sustainable and it definitely is not a top choice for bread lovers! For some people, it is a good "jump start" to lose weight before transitioning to a more sustainable nutrition pattern. Whether you mix and match or create your own "Selfitarian" plan, pick something that will work for you over the long run. All girls want to look healthy, be healthy, and enjoy a well-lived life with few health issues.

We've covered how to get strong bones, build our muscles, hydrate our skin and reviewed nutrition plans to improve our health. Now on to the fun part of perfecting our hair and makeup!

# HAIR and MAKEUP

## Secrets the French Women Know

I once dated a man from France, and he was AMAZED at how American women tend to follow whatever the latest fad or trend happens to be. Many fashions or makeup trends may look fabulous on some women and truly unflattering on others. His point was that women should be independent thinkers, know what their strongest points are, and really focus on them, no matter the latest trend.

I succumbed to trends in the past until I realized they were not always flattering to me. That neon orange color did NOTHING for my skin tone. A polo shirt makes me look ten to twenty pounds heavier. I love a smokey eye, but on me, I look more Goth than great. So, I appreciated his viewpoint. Although, it is not always easy to figure out our best traits. It can take some trial and error.

The first thing you need to do is figure out what clothes flatter your figure. You may look great in a polo shirt, unfortunately, I did not. Sheath dresses look good on me, and I have a whole closet full! I kept thinking I should vary them with A-line dresses or dresses with a fuller skirt, but they just don't look as good. Think of some of the famous actresses and what they wear. Sophia Vergara consistently wears the same style. Why, because it flatters her figure. If you have a little waist, cinch it! A perky booty, then emphasize it. Great upper arms, it is only short sleeves for you! Look for a celebrity who has a similar figure type as you do and then look at their images to see what style they wear and what looks best. Then try the same styles on yourself!

The next thing is to find colors that flatter your skin tone. You might need to take a color quiz or read about how to determine the best colors for you. Orange in general is not a flattering color for me, but if it is a gold-orange color, I can pull it off. Consider colors not only for your clothes but also for your makeup. Is the blackest black the best mascara for you or will the soft brown make your eyes more mesmerizing?

If you are not sure, try going for free makeovers at the cosmetics counters. You can test out different colors and think about them. You may feel some pressure to make a purchase, but you can respond with "I'd like to wear it for a while and see how it looks in different lighting before I make a purchase" and you DO want to check it out in natural lighting and not just the fluorescent lighting in the store. Lipsticks can vary so much. One red may look okay whereas another will make your teeth look super white and be a focus point.

You'll want to decide what is your very best feature. Enlist your friends too. I had a best girlfriend that used to go shopping with me. We'd ask each other how an outfit looked. If it was not "super fab" then it was a kind way to say you needed to pass on it.

You may have incredible eyes, high cheekbones, a cupid's bow mouth, or fantastic hair. Whatever is your strongest feature, that is the one to master to perfection! This is what my former beau was talking about. French women know how to dress for their figure type and definitely understand their best facial features and create an intriguing aura.

Another secret is that French women exude confidence and feel they are beautiful. It doesn't matter if they are a natural beauty or have a fantastic figure. Have you ever met someone who wasn't all that pretty or had a figure that was not the typical American ideal, yet the woman had such a presence and was a man magnet? It is because that woman is self-assured and that is very sexy.

You say you are not that self-confident? Well, you can fake it until you make it! When I first started speaking to large groups at work, I was a nervous Nellie. I would practice in front of the mirror for hours. I got butterflies and my mouth became a desert. But I HAD to be self-assured and be a leader people wanted to follow. I used to pretend that I was Miss America going on stage and would Miss America stutter and look like a deer in the headlights? No! It helped me "fake it" until I did get over my butterflies and speaking engagements became second nature to me. You can do the same thing! You can pretend to be self-confident and tell yourself you look fantastic. And guess what? Others will see you the same way! So, find the right style of clothing for you, pick colors that enhance your skin tone, and master the one feature that will captivate others. The French women aren't the only ones keeping the secret today!

## Lipstick that Sticks All Day!

Working in the hectic world of healthcare, I would look fabulous at the start of the day, but by midday my lipstick was gone, my hair was starting to deflate or fall out of the bun, and my face was getting shiny. While I could blot my face and use some emergency hair spray to get me through the day the biggest issue was finding lipstick that stayed on! Even when not at work, who wants fading lipstick on a date? It seemed that more lipstick got on my glass than stayed on my lips! It took a while, but I finally solved the disappearing lipstick puzzle.

The trick is not to buy lipstick, but a lip stain! Lip stains stay on MUCH longer. You may even have a perfect pink pout when you wake up after being a sleeping beauty. Yes, some lip stains stay on FOREVER. It can be good or bad depending on if you made a mistake putting it on. You can't put your lip stain on while in traffic!

So, you are wondering where to buy a lip stain? Almost all makeup companies make lip stains with some being more durable than others. SeneGence makes a great lip stain. Who? You say you've never heard of SeneGence. SeneGence uses reps that you can find online. It is like Avon or Mary Kay in how they market and distribute their products. They even have a product called "Oops" to remove the lip stain from your skin if you draw outside the lines. Another favorite of mine is Loreal Infallible. It is not marketed as a lip stain, but rather a "long-lasting lip transfer-proof lipstick" (sounds like a lip stain to me). Beauty magazine reviewers loved it too!

So, you're thinking, "Sign me up for lip stains!" One drawback is that because they do STICK to your lips, they can also be very drying. Some lip stains are packaged as a two-step process. Step 1 is putting on the lip stain and Step 2 is applying a moisturizer or "glossy" finish that hydrates your lips.

I ALWAYS use lip moisturizer. Whether you grab a budget-friendly Chap Stick or splurge for a luxe, high-end product, you'll want to use it after applying the lip stain, throughout the day, and before you lay your head down to sleep. Another tip is to look for a lip moisturizer that has SPF. You want to protect that pout from the sun!

## I Want Luscious Lashes

Eyelashes can really draw a person into your eyes and make them melt. It can also focus a person on your eyes and away from a part of you that may not be as flattering. Have you ever wondered how many eyelashes you have? We average about 100 lashes on the lower lid and 200 or more on the upper lid. The lashes tend to be longer in the middle. Every girl wants big, beautiful eyes and long, luscious lashes are a must-do! But how do I get my lashes to the luscious level? All girls know about mascara and it is a start.

Did you know that mascara was created in 1913 by the French? Maybelline made it popular in the United States in 1917. We can thank Mabel William's pharmacist brother for taking her homemade coal and Vaseline concoction and producing a cake mascara! He eventually renamed the company to Maybelline in her honor.

We've come a long way since those early versions. Today, there are innumerable brands, a variety of colors and wands that help to lengthen and curl. You may already have your favorite brand. I've tried a lot, and in my opinion, nothing compares to Estee Lauder's mascara. A good runner-up is Loreal's Lash Paradise. But mascara alone is not enough.

I like to prepare my lashes with a lash curler. Yes, it seems crazy to curl your lashes with a contraption that looks like it could hurt you. And yes, you need to position it correctly to not pull your eyelid, but it helps. I also like eyeliner as I feel it helps to define the lash line and make my eyes pop more. I use a variety of shades, sometimes just a basic black while other times I'll use navy or green to match the blue and green in my eyes.

Look at your eyes and see if there are colors you want to bring out such as gray or copper flecks in your eyes. Not sure or confused and don't want to buy five different eyeliner colors to try? Getting a makeover at a beauty counter is a great way to test out different eyeliner colors. Let the makeup artist know that you are interested in eyeliner but aren't sure what color would look best. While I usually feel pressure to buy something after an hour-long session, I have learned to say, "Let me think about it", unless I was planning on making a purchase anyway.

Have you heard of an amazing product called lash primer? The primer will lengthen and thicken your lashes and "prep" them for mascara. And oh my, does it work! Some mascaras may come with "Step 1 and Step 2" in which case, the primer is Step 1. Or you can buy a separate lash primer. Remember to use waterproof products if you are going to be in the water so you will maintain your captivating look versus looking like a raccoon.

Other ways to have longer lashes include lash serums. Some condition instead of lengthening. The lengthening versions usually contain bimatoprost which is an eye drop used by people who suffer from glaucoma. A side effect is that it grows eyelashes longer! It is applied with a tiny brush along the lash line. Have you heard of Latisse? Guess what the active ingredient is? Yes, bimatoprost. It requires a prescription and is effective if used correctly. If you are interested in using a bimatoprost product, keep in mind that Latisse is not your only option. Budget-conscious girls can find it at a much lower price by doing a little research.

Should you "fake it until you make it" with false lashes or extensions? Maybe. Gluing "falsies" onto my eyelid was never very appealing to me. I would buy the lashes but could never figure out the technical aspects for them to look and feel good. If you can make it work, go for it! A professional can help with extensions if you want to splurge. Keep in mind that you don't want to go too long. Some girls overdo it and look like they have spiders on their eyes. Avoid the spidey look, you don't want to scare anyone off!

## Can I Do My Own Blowout?

You might wonder if you can do your own blowout and the answer is – Yes, absolutely! Now unless you are an octopus, trying to handle a round hairbrush and hairdryer can be tricky. The good news is that there are many versions of an airbrush out there. These are hairdryers that have a very large, round brush or curling attachments that you use to dry and either curl or straighten your hair at the same time. They work great, especially for straightening your hair.

The price range can vary from $50 or less to over $500. The high-end, such as the Dyson Air Wrap version has the technology to prevent frizziness, flyaways and protects hair from extreme heat, and dries hair faster. The Dyson Air Wrap measures heat flow forty times a second (yes, I said each second)! The budget versions such as Conair or Revlon while not as tech-savvy, work well too.

A few pre-drying tips include not using too much conditioner after you shampoo. A little bit on the ends or the bottom half of your locks is all you need. It is always wise to use a hair protector before drying your hair. If your airbrush dryer claims not to do any heat damage, you still want a product to help detangle, protect your hair from UVA/UVB rays, and infuse some shine.

A heat protectant also keeps colored hair looking true and prevents brassiness from developing. A few sprays are all you need. If you go overboard, your hair may end up feeling (and looking) a bit greasy. If I want to add volume to my hair, I use a root volumizer. I'm not sure what is in it, but you spray it on your hair when it is wet and the lifting you do with the airbrush does the trick. No more flat, helmet hair!

I find the airbrushes do a fantastic job of smoothing your hair and infusing volume. Some claim to produce flowing, wavy curls and I'm not sure if it is user-error or they just don't perform as well as a curling iron. I have straight hair, so it might be they work better with girls who already have some curl to work with!

Ideally, you'll select an airbrush with a variety of heat settings. A little-known secret is that the cold setting helps to set your style, infuses shine, and locks the cuticle. Hmm, sounds like it takes the place of shine spray and hair spray. Sort of and we want as few products on our hair as possible. We want it to be shiny, sexy hair we can put our hands through without it being sticky or breaking from using too much hair spray!

Now, you don't have to totally dry your hair using the cold setting. You can use a medium temperature to get it around 70% dry, then switch to the cool setting to finish drying and styling your hair. Another pro-tip is to section your hair into four or five sections and dry one section at a time starting at the bottom and working your way up. You can "rough dry" your hair with the airbrush initially before sectioning it and focusing on those lovely locks.

Once your hair is sectioned, you can really get to work. If your airbrush has different brush styles, you can pick the one that works best for the style you want. Smaller brush barrels will create tighter curls and a larger barrel will create more volume and waves. Think about your curling iron and the results you get with different-sized barrels.

The key is working on small sections at a time, approximately one-inch sections. Pay attention after you get your haircut to what your hairdresser is doing and how they are styling your hair. The hairdresser makes it look so easy! You want to replicate the process with your airbrush. You can finish with a light hair spray or a SMALL amount of finishing cream if you tend to have frizzy hair.

Another tip is if you wake up with bedhead hair and want those locks to look fabulous and not fatigued, spritz your hair with some water and grab your airbrush! Yes, it will bring your hair back to life without having to jump in the shower to shampoo and condition it first. Everyone knows that your day will be great no matter what happens if you are having a "good hair day." Here's to EVERY girl having a good hair day every day!

## Should I Dye My Hair?

This is a question that many women ask themselves. Many girls consider having a different shade of hair color at one point or another. Do blondes really have more fun? Would I look sexy as a fiery redhead? Will that chestnut make my eyes pop? How will that raven-black look on me? Stunning or more like Elvira? Should I embrace my gray hair? Are highlights a better choice for me? There is no right or wrong answer. Hair color is a personal preference. Here are some tips to help you, so you don't make an "Oh my goodness, can we fix it?" mistake.

First, consider your skin tone and eye color. Look at pictures of women who have a similar skin tone and what hair color compliments their skin tone? Do you have warm or cool skin undertones? Look at the back of your hand in natural light. Do your veins look blue? If so, you have cool undertones. More green? Then you have warm undertones. Uh, they look both blue and green. You are neutral!

There are also apps where you can upload a photo and "try on" different hair colors. Other options include going to a wig shop and trying on different wigs. You can see different hair colors and styles!

Take a trusted girlfriend with you to help with the analysis of whether it is a Yes, No, or Maybe. Consulting with your hairstylist about what color they think would look good on you is always beneficial. They are experts and understand what colors can be achieved and what would look great with your skin tone and eyes!

If you plan on the DIY route, you might want to try a semi-permanent dye to lighten or darken a few shades or slightly change your hair color. Semi-permanent is the key word. It eventually washes out if you don't like it. Lightening your hair can be tricky, especially if you are a medium brown or deeper shade. Becoming a blonde or even highlighting can require a two-step process or the addition of "drabbers" to control brassiness. Many a woman ended up with yellow or orange tones that were overpowering and not at all flattering. You want to be a bombshell and not a clown!

Do you love your white or silver hair, but find it looks more like dull pewter or has an icky yellowed look? How can we prevent this from happening? We want that silver hair to shine and reflect light! Remember to wear a hat if you are out in the sun to prevent damage. The sun can also turn your pretty white locks yellow. If they are yellowish, a purple shampoo or conditioner can brighten them. Look for leave-in or detangling spray that also provides UVA and UVB protection. Gray hair tends to be coarse and may look dull. Don't skimp on your conditioning treatments! You need to hydrate your hair. Use a little hair serum after getting out of the shower. Hair serums have oil as an ingredient and provide the shine you need!

## I Like Brass Bands, Not Brassy Hair!

Are you a blonde or brunette who ended up with unwanted yellow, orange, or red tones with your hair color transformation? Is your gray hair looking blah versus saying wow? Gray and silver hair can look dull or end up with the same yellow tones that can beleaguer your blonde sisters. Even brunettes can end up with orange or red undertones that distract from their brown beauty. To reduce or eliminate these unwanted, unflattering yellow, orange, or red tones, you want to use a purple or blue shampoo.

Purple shampoos can reduce the brassiness of yellow tones, as well as brighten blonde and silver hair so it shines. Okay, you think you've seen purple shampoos and may even be using one, but what is a blue shampoo and when would you use it? You've never even heard of blue shampoo. Blue shampoos help minimize and eliminate red and orange brassy colors that tend to affect brunettes.

You might be wondering where you can find a purple or blue shampoo. Purple shampoos are easy to find and popular. Drug and discount stores usually carry several brands. Blue shampoos are not as readily available unless you go to a beauty supply store or search online.

While these shampoos can do the trick by reducing brassiness and refreshing your color, they can be really drying to your strands. Start using them once a week to get rid of the brass and to refresh. Then use a hydrating, non-sulfate shampoo on other days. Some ladies dilute their purple or blue shampoo by mixing it in with their regular shampoo. There are a lot of ways to use them and keep your hair looking absolutely beautiful!

## Create a Home Spa – Discover Your Lovely Locks

Let's continue with the pampering at home! Whether you choose to have a full day of beauty or break up your pampering sessions, don't forget to set the mood with spa music, aromatherapy, and infused water that we reviewed in Create a Home Spa – Set the Tone! Now let's create gorgeous, lustrous hair and get those nails done!

Decide on your hair potion before shampooing. Keep in mind that conditioners are used after shampooing, whereas reconstructors are applied and work their magic before you shampoo your hair. There is a plethora of deep hair conditioners you can select. A deep hair conditioner provides moisture and helps protect your hair with heat styling. They can be used once a week.

Hair reconstructors contain protein. They restore the structure of the hair and work inside the hair shaft to repair it. They work differently from deep hair conditioners and can be used once a month. Too frequent use of a hair reconstructor can have the opposite effect and cause breakage. Whichever product you use give your scalp a lovely scalp massage when you shampoo! If you color your hair, double-check that your shampoo is free of sulfates and color-safe.

Apply your favorite hair potion then place a plastic shower cap on your head. Heat helps these products work better. If you have a bonnet-style hair dryer or one you can sit under, then grab your fave magazine and sit under the hair dryer. If you only have a handheld hair dryer or none, you can go sit outside if it is warm or put a towel on your head. If you are feeling energetic, then you can exercise while you have the shower cap on!

Rinse your hair after the recommended time and let it dry naturally. If you can stand rinsing with cold water, it helps to close the shaft and increase shine! It takes some time and bravery to get used to rinsing with cold water. Burr! A little bit of hair serum adds shine and protects your hair. A word of caution, if you go overboard with the serum your hair may look too shiny and like the fake hair on mannequins!

If you must use a hair dryer to dry your hair, be sure to use a heat protectant. If you have a choice of settings, switching to the cooler setting will help. If you are in a rush, switch to a cooler setting when your hair is at the "almost dry" phase. Whether you put your soft, shiny glorious hair into a ponytail, straighten, or curl it, enjoy it and have a GREAT hair day!

## Create a Home Spa – DIY Mani/Pedi

Next is the mani/pedi. Yes, you can do it yourself! First, remove any existing nail polish and then use clippers and a nail file to shape your nails. Emery boards or crystal nail files work best. Remember to file your nails only in one direction to avoid breaks. If your feet are calloused, a pumice stone will work wonders to get your feet back to being baby soft!

Now, let's take care of those pesky cuticles. And the best way to get rid of overgrown cuticles is to start by softening them. After removing any existing nail polish, let's soak those fingers and toes. You can heat some water and add some essential oil. Tea tree oil, peppermint, or lavender are good choices. There are therapeutic foot soaks with Epsom salt that have essential oils in them. Other soak options include using nourishing oils, moisturizing lotion, or even dish soap. Choose your ingredients, relax, and soak for 5–10 minutes. A foot spa is a splurge but can be "Oh So Relaxing." Household bowls can be used to soak your nails.

Once you have soaked, apply a cuticle remover to your cuticles. There are cream and liquid versions. Sally Hansen is cost-effective and does the job. Leave it on for the allotted time, then remove it per instructions. Push back your cuticles with an orange stick or metal tool. Once you have your cuticles in tip-top shape, then you can soften and moisturize your fingers and toes.

There are several ways to soften your hands and feet. You may choose to do this after your soak. Exfoliating scrubs work wonders. Everyone has probably experienced the Mary Kay "Satin Hands" process. It is a bestseller and delivers results! There are other scrubs out there as well. Any "scrub" has exfoliating properties and can be used not only on your hands and feet but also on the rest of your body. On a tight budget? No problem, you can create your own scrub at home for pennies. Do-it-yourself versions start with an oil such as olive or coconut oil. Then you add an exfoliating agent such as sugar, coffee, brown sugar, or sea salt. Mix it up and scrub away!

If you are going to paint your nails, you will need to prep them after all this pampering so the nail polish will adhere! Wipe your nails with nail polish remover or alcohol. You can apply traditional nail polish or invest in gel nail polish which requires a UV lamp. I like gel nail polish. It strengthens the nails and stays on for weeks! I've been amazed at how healthy my nails look when the gel nail polish is removed.

The only downside is REMOVING the gel nail polish. You'll need to rough your nail polish up with an emery board and soak your nails in acetone. Since the gel really sticks, it can take up to fifteen minutes for the acetone to start to dissolve. If you do choose to go the traditional nail polish route, be sure to use a base coat. Otherwise, your nails can turn a yellow color that resembles a werewolf's nails!

Now that you are absolutely glowing, enjoy yourself! Style your hair, marvel at your luminous skin, and life is ALWAYS better when your nails are painted. Whether you are staying in to read that new novel or the latest magazine, watching a show on television, or getting ready to let the world see you, let your beauty and serenity shine. You ARE fabulous, inside and out!

## I Want Big, Beautiful Eyes!

It has been said that the eyes are the window to the soul. Our eyes are how we see the world and express ourselves, and tend to be a focal point when interacting with others. Bigger eyes make us look alert and more engaging. So, we want mesmerizing eyes!

No matter the color or shape of your eyes, there are tips to make those peepers REALLY peep! Every picture needs a frame and the frame for our gorgeous eyes is your eyebrows. You don't want them to be too thin, but we don't want a jungle up there either. Keep your eyebrows trimmed and an eyebrow pencil can do WONDERS to fill in gaps, help to frame your eyes, and add some color if you are fair or have gray in your eyebrows.

We want to minimize or eliminate puffiness and dark circles, which do nothing but make you look tired and dragged out. I recommend trying to avoid getting these in the first place. Limiting sodium and alcohol can prevent puffiness. Getting your beauty sleep DOES help you look more beautiful! Think of your 10 pm lights out as another beauty treatment. And this beauty treatment not only helps your complexion but also your cognition, cortisol levels, sense of well-being, and heart health!

Let's not forget about hydrating our bodies and using our SPF before going outside. Eyestrain can contribute to dark circles. How many of us sit in front of a screen for hours a day? Whether it is working in front of a computer or scrolling on our phone or tablet, all that screen time can strain our eyes. Try to take breaks and look away from the screen every thirty minutes. It really does help.

Now, some girls may be genetically prone to having dark circles and we tend to develop dark circles as we age. Certain eye medicines can cause dark circles three to six months after starting treatment and this includes lash lengthening serums such as Latisse. Are you feeling tired, lightheaded, or maybe short of breath? These are some of the symptoms of anemia. A study of people with peri-orbital hyperpigmentation, also known as dark circles under the eyes, found that 50% of the participants had anemia and when it was treated their dark circles disappeared. When was the last time you had your blood levels checked?

So, you are getting your eight hours of beauty sleep, hydrating with eight glasses or more of water a day, giving up the nightly glass of wine, getting your blood levels checked, using your SPF, and STILL having dark circles. There are a few other ideas to consider. Sleeping with your head on an extra pillow may help. Cold compresses are a welcome relief for the eyes. Who hasn't seen a girl at a spa with cold cucumbers on her eyes? You can also use a cold washcloth or chill black or green tea bags in water and apply for ten to twenty minutes. You can keep a supply in the fridge for easy access. And of course, there is always concealer and makeup to cover them up.

Additional tips to create a bigger, more beautiful look include using eyeliner only on the outer portion of your lower lashes. If you use it on the entire lower lash line, it makes your eyes look smaller! You can line your entire eyelid with eyeliner but keep it thin until you get to the outer portion. Make the line thicker at the outer portion. This technique will bring out your natural beauty. A cat eye at the end also helps to make the eye look bigger.

Choose an eyeliner that complements the color of your eyes. Consider plum eyeliner if you have green eyes, a coppery brown to make blue eyes pop, violet shades for brown eyes, and royal blue for the gray-eyed goddesses! There is always basic black too. If you highlight the inner corner of your eyelid after applying your eyeshadow, you'll say, "Wow," at how your eyes pop. A little shimmer there makes a world of difference. Try it and I'm sure you'll like it!

For the final touch, we want long, lovely lashes. We want volume and length. If you aren't using a lash curler, you might want to start using one. I know they look like an instrument of torture, and it can be a bit of a struggle to figure out how to place it to get the right curl, but it does lift and curl your lashes prepping them for the next step. I always use a lash prep product to lengthen and thicken before applying my mascara. It seems to double the length of my lashes. Who needs falsies when you can lengthen your own lashes?

Then I select the perfect mascara. Most of the time I go with black mascara. I've tried blue, green, and violet colors that really didn't do anything but make people stare at my eyes and ask, "Are you wearing purple mascara?" Hmm, I wanted to look alluring, not odd! There are hundreds of mascaras out there at all different price points. Try a few and find the perfect one for your lashes! Another tip is to make your lashes a little thicker and longer at the outer eye to magically create a more doe-like look.

We're looking and feeling good. There is one more area that is essential to feeling fantastic: self-care! Sometimes it is very hard to find time to focus on ourselves. Read ahead to find out why it is so important and how you CAN fit it into a busy lifestyle.

# SELF CARE

# I Want to Be a Sleeping Beauty!

There are not many luxuries better than a fabulous night's sleep where you wake up refreshed, wide-eyed, and ready to jump out of bed and into your day! Sleep is SO important to your health: physical, mental, and cognitive. How much sleep do you need? The National Institutes of Health states that adults need 7–9 hours of sleep a night. About 41% of people sleep less than 7 hours a night.

However, if you are a woman who has PMS, menstruating, pregnant, in the postpartum phase, peri- or post-menopausal, your numbers are much more dismal. These women experience sleep disturbances and/or poor sleep quality up to 75% of the time! As we age, we tend to sleep less and experience an increase in sleep disturbances. Are you in one of these groups and not getting enough good quality sleep?

Not sleeping well affects your body in many ways. Ever wonder why you seem so hungry after sleeping poorly? Your appetite hormones get out of balance when deprived of sleep. The appetite-suppressing one (leptin) is reduced and the appetite-stimulating one (ghrelin) is increased. This is not what we want to happen! Glucose intolerance can occur and people who sleep less than five hours a night have a 2 ½ times greater risk of becoming diabetic.

The risk of having a heart attack or stroke also increases with people who sleep poorly. Your cortisol levels and blood pressure increase and your body experiences more inflammation. Your mental health suffers too. Depression, anxiety, irritability, over-reacting, and low self-esteem are associated with lack of sleep. In addition, your memory and cognitive function suffer as well. Who hasn't felt dragged out and experienced brain fog after sleeping poorly?

What happens to your body when you sleep at night? Your body goes into a repair and recovery cycle. Your body conserves energy and there are several processes occurring "behind the curtain". For example, your brain shifts gears and removes toxins. Hormones are created and cells have time to repair and regrow. This includes muscle and tissue repair and growth. You WANT to see results from your exercise and strength training routine! Immune cells and antibodies are created during sleep. No wonder I got sick when I was sleeping poorly! Okay, you get it and want to get your seven hours of beauty sleep but sometimes struggle to fall asleep or stay asleep.

There are sleep hygiene tips that can greatly increase your ability to fall asleep and stay asleep. Sleep Dynamics talks about the 10-3-2-1-0 rule. You say you've never heard of it? Neither did I, but it makes a lot of sense. At least ten hours before your bedtime avoid caffeine, limit food and alcohol three hours before (I know, alcohol helps you doze off, but it impacts the quality of your sleep, so it isn't really helping), stop working two hours before bed and turn off the screen (phone, tablet, tv, etc.) an hour before and hit the snooze button zero times. Oh no, you LOVE the snooze button. Unfortunately, the snooze button is not good for your REM sleep, and we want the BEST sleep possible.

Other tips include having a cooler bedroom, using blackout curtains or a sleep mask, and not having blue light in your bedroom. You're asking what is blue light? Blue light can come from an alarm clock, cell phone, cable box, or TV and can disturb your circadian rhythm. Blue light makes us alert and in a "wake" mode. Blue light is great in the morning but can inhibit our sleep at night. If you really like your NetFlix at night, you can invest in blue light glasses to wear in the evening. These glasses with amber lenses filter the blue light from the environment. You can even order prescription blue light glasses!

As I've gotten older, I have become more sensitive to blue light. I do not have an alarm clock in my bedroom, cover the cable box light, and use my sleep mask. I wear my blue light glasses if I want to watch TV close to bedtime. Check your phone, it may have an amber setting where it reduces blue light in the evening and night hours. Another consideration, if you live in a noisy household or neighborhood, is earplugs! And go to bed at a set time, maybe 10 pm?

Other tips include avoiding nicotine. Your body will wake up after three or four hours as it is going through nicotine withdrawal. Get your strenuous exercise done earlier in the day. Avoid daytime naps and if you MUST nap, do so for only 20–30 minutes. If you find a bath relaxing, jump in the tub for a few luxurious minutes before bedtime.

Some people swear by "heavenly beds." These are super soft beds that feel like you are on a cloud, usually with high thread count linens. You can create your own with soft pillows, a mattress topper, and super soft linens. If you are on a budget, bamboo sheets are soft and less expensive than 1,000-thread count linens. Other ways to relax include lavender aromatherapy. You can use a diffuser, or a favorite of mine is pillow spray! Chamomile tea or warm milk can help promote drowsiness.

What about melatonin? Your body naturally produces melatonin at night. Web MD reports that short-term melatonin supplementation is safe, especially if you are experiencing jet lag, working an off shift, or are experiencing insomnia. Another option is drinking tart cherry juice before bed. It contains tryptophan and melatonin. Tryptophan is an essential amino acid that gets converted into serotonin which is associated with better sleep.

You've probably experienced the effects of tryptophan and didn't even know it. Turkey contains tryptophan. No wonder you get drowsy after eating turkey on Thanksgiving! When selecting tart cherry juice, choose one without added sugar. Keep in mind that it will be very tart! Some girls like to make a spritzer by mixing 3–4 ounces of the juice with sparkling water or club soda and adding a splash of lime. A great option if you're having difficulty getting to sleep or wake up in the middle of the night and are WIDE awake.

Since melatonin can interact with other drugs or aggravate health conditions, it is best to check with your practitioner before using it. If you have incorporated these sleep hygiene tips and are not seeing results or think you may have a more serious sleep disorder, reach out to your practitioner as there may be diagnostic tests or other interventions that you may need. Sleep well, my lovely, and wake up to an absolutely beautiful day!

## No Woman is an Island

You might be wondering what I mean by "no woman is an island?" We are surrounded by people and often we are caregivers to our children and others in our lives. What I am referring to is not how we care for others, but how we let others care for us. Women are programmed to be caring, loving, helpful, and defer their own needs for their partner or family. We are very good at offering help and not always as good at accepting it.

The modern girl is taught to be independent and self-sufficient. We don't NEED a man or a partner, rather it is our choice to have one. We can do it all or so it seems. A secret that smart girls know is they CAN do it all, just not all at once. We need to choose what is a priority and focus on those aspects of our life. It could be our career, home life, living a healthy lifestyle, or improving the community. And those priorities can change as we make our journey through life.

Being able to fend for ourselves is a positive but it can also make it difficult to ask for or even accept help when it is offered. How many times have you said, "No, it's okay. I can do it." This could be taking on an extra project at work, baking a dozen cupcakes the night before for a school event, or adding a few errands to an already busy day. Many times, others are willing to help, but we don't want to "bother" people or have them go out of their way. The consequence of not asking for or accepting help is that it can increase your stress and cortisol levels. This causes inflammation in your body that can have very negative effects if sustained over time. Yikes, trying to be "nice" could actually be killing you!

What we don't realize is that other people WANT to help us. I truly did not understand this until a very healthy family member became ill and was hospitalized. Others and I desperately wanted to help this person with ANYTHING we could do after she was released from the hospital. It was frustrating when she was declining help and felt she could do things herself. Finally, she slowly started to accept help.

I kept thinking, "That would be me," and it IS me in many instances. For example, I've spent hours researching auto mechanics when I could have asked my "car guy" acquaintance who he uses or recommends. I frantically ran out to the grocery store for a forgotten vegetable when having a guest over versus asking if the guest could pick up the broccoli on the way over as he passed the grocery store. I held onto yardwork remains for weeks filling my two barrels every week for a month instead of asking a neighbor if I could borrow their blue barrels the first week and put all of it curbside. Crazy, isn't it?! Why did I do it? I didn't want to bother anyone and felt I should be self-sufficient. In each of these instances, each person would have been thrilled to loan me a few barrels, give me advice, or contribute to a dinner.

We need to reframe our thinking and start asking for help when needed and accepting it when offered. Practice saying, "Could I ask a favor?", "Yes, please" and "Thank you" versus the automatic "No thank you. I'm okay" or "I can do it." Remember that it makes people feel good to help someone, especially when they are asking how they can help! Whether it is offering advice when asked, lending a tool to make a project easier, or borrowing a stick of butter when in a cooking emergency, we need to learn to reach out and share in each other's knowledge and resources.

It can be a difficult paradigm shift. Sometimes, the start is just realizing you could have asked for help and thinking, "Next time I will!" If you are thinking, "This is not me at all. I am not shy at ALL about asking for help," then you have mastered a skill that not every woman has achieved. In that case, spread the word and help your other sisters realize that no woman is an island!

## Feel Good in 15 Minutes

Feeling sluggish, a little blue, or just blah? Let's fix that in fifteen minutes! Not with a glass of wine, but rather with fifteen minutes of exercise, laughter, or singing. All three work to help you feel good whether done together or separately. Did you know that all three are forms of aerobic exercise and release endorphins? We know we increase our oxygen consumption during exercise, the same thing happens when we laugh or sing too!

So, what are endorphins? Endorphins are feel-good chemicals that help you feel energized and uplifted. When you feel good, you strengthen your immune system. Exercise, laughter, and singing help to relax tension, improve the quality of your sleep, reduce blood pressure, and exercise your muscles. There are many ways to exercise besides the treadmill and weights.

How about a walk in nature or with Fido? Not feeling like getting out of the house? What about a dance-off or creating a fun cheer? Tell your audience (okay, it might just be your kitty) to give you a "Let's", then say, "Get Energized!" You might just start laughing at yourself too. Have you ever laughed so hard that your tummy hurt? That happens when I get together with my sister and I have to say, "Stop, my tummy hurts" as I am laughing. What a fun way to exercise your core!

Singing helps to work your diaphragm, respiratory, abdominal, facial, leg, and back muscles. Who knew? Singing is so easy to do and portable! Frustrated in traffic, start singing to your favorite tunes. Not so happy while cleaning the house? Pump it up with some tunes, and did that Swiffer duster just turn into a microphone? So, when you are not feeling 100%, get outside for a walk or run, put on some Diana

Ross and belt it out or listen to your favorite comedian to feel MUCH better in fifteen minutes!

## Attracting What You Want!

Do you want a better body, a more interesting job, or a new boyfriend? Yes, yes, I do, you say. While there isn't a magic lamp you can rub for a genie to emerge and grant your wishes, there are ways to attract what you want. First of all, you need to think positively. If you see the glass as half-full, it will be easier than if you are a glass-half-empty type of girl. Instead of thinking about what won't happen, such as "I'm never going to find a job I like," shift your thinking to what you want to happen, "I'm going to find a job I love."

This is a shift to what is possible and creates positive energy. If you have a negative thought, immediately think about how you can change it to a positive one. If you are not used to thinking in this manner, you may not even realize when you are thinking negatively. Ask your friends to remind you to change your thinking if any negative phrases come out of your mouth.

Next, you need to believe and feel what you want to attract. In your mind imagine what you want as a goal or what you want to achieve. Visualization is extremely powerful in helping people achieve their goals. Exercise videos routinely incorporate visualization techniques. I noticed this during my video exercise routine. As I am finishing a set, the trainer keeps telling me to "visualize what you want your buns to look like" to keep me motivated and focused. And it does help me to power through the routine! For visualization to be especially effective, you need to engage all of your senses: sight, hearing, taste, touch, and smell.

Narrow down what your office or job space would look like. Don't forget the details! What colors are the walls and rug? When you look around you, what do you see? Are there paintings on the wall, peers working, the outdoors, or a kitchen? What noises do you hear? Is it a cacophony of voices or noises, is music playing or is it peaceful and quiet? Engage your sense of touch. How does it feel sitting in your chair, imagine the fabric and type of clothing you'd be wearing, if using tools are they rough or smooth? What temperature is your work environment? Is there an air conditioning draft? Are you outside in stifling hot air or is there a refreshing breeze?

You can even imagine smell and taste! Is there aromatherapy in your space or are you outdoors smelling city traffic or jasmine? Can you smell the coffee and how would it taste? Would you be bringing your lunch? Is lunch a crunchy salad with tangy Italian dressing, a salami-and-Swiss-cheese sandwich on soft potato bread or would you be heating up last night's spaghetti?

It may seem silly, but the more you can imagine your space and your experiences, the more effective it becomes. Visualization improves goal setting and motivation, focuses your concentration, and improves your confidence! In addition, it activates neural pathways. Think of the many successful athletes who incorporated visualization into their training programs. The world-famous golfer Jack Nicklaus has stated he never hit a ball, not even in practice, without visualizing how he wanted the shot to go. Michael Phelps, the all-time most medal-winning Olympian, used visualization day and night to imagine everything from getting on the swimming block, to swimming and celebrating his win afterwards. He received 22 medals, with 18 of them being gold. I'd say visualization is worth a shot!

The third step, which can be the hardest, is taking action. It would be nice if we could think positively and visualize what we wanted then, poof, it occurred. Unfortunately, it is not that easy. Those are precursors to doing the hard work and can make it much more successful when you do act. Think about how you would go about getting that fantastic job. Do you need training or education? Can you obtain it remotely or do you need in-classroom time? Do you need to network, join chat rooms, or search specific job boards? Are there volunteer or intern opportunities to get your foot in the door? Do you know anyone who is in the field that you could talk to about strategy tips or is willing to mentor you?

Creating a to-do list can be very helpful. Brainstorm and write down all your ideas. Review your list and prioritize what you can easily do and then follow through. As you gain more knowledge, you may readjust your priorities or decide a different direction is needed. This is a dynamic process that will most likely be fluid. Go with the flow! Engage your friends and family to keep you on track, assist with course correction, and provide positive reinforcement for the many little successes you'll achieve along the way. Keep your sense of humor! Not every idea or action will be a hit. If you can still laugh when something bombs and learn from it, you'll be on the right path. Remember it is a journey. Keep visualizing as you make progress and advance towards your goal and before long you will attract what you want!

## What We Can Learn from Blue Zones

Some of you may know what a blue zone is while others may ask, "What is a Blue Zone"? A blue zone is a geographic area, usually a town or city, where a disproportionate number of people live up to 100 years or older and are healthy. The centenarians are physically active and free of dementia.

The blue zones have been identified in Costa Rica, Japan, Greece, Italy, and the United States. You may already be living in one! So, what can we learn about living from the blue zones that will help us be happy, healthy, and able to live a long life? Most of it is information that we already know, and it is worth repeating as it REALLY makes a difference!

We need to stay physically active, and this doesn't mean an hour at the gym a few times a week. We want to incorporate physical activity into our daily routine and lifestyle. Walk or bike when you can. Do you need a gallon of milk or some eggs? Walk or bike to the grocery store and pick it up. I pick providers (dentist, primary care physician, beautician, etc.) that are within a mile of my house so I can walk to my appointments.

Gardening, housework, and even doing laundry are physical activities that help move our joints. My motto is "If it is good exercise, I will do it myself." So yes, I mow my own grass and clean my own house even though I could pay someone else to do it. A tip is to break up the activities.

Few people have three or four hours on a weekend to clean the house. Try doing one or two rooms a day for ten or fifteen minutes. It isn't that hard to clean a bathroom during the day or evening. After doing the dishes, clean the countertops, wipe down the cabinets, mop the floor, and voila! the kitchen is done. Get the vacuum out and go crazy before watching a movie or your favorite show. If you are not into lawn work or cleaning, think of other ways you can get daily exercise in. Walking the dog in the morning and evening, cooking without using pre-cut food or the food processor, folding laundry, raking leaves, shoveling snow, parking as far away as possible from the store, and taking the steps. It all adds up!

I'm sure you are already thinking that processed foods are a no-no, and you are correct! Blue zone inhabitants eat primarily a plant-based diet with limited amounts of meat and eat until they are 80% full. Fill your plate with tasty fruits and vegetables or have delicious, seasoned soup.

Many people in Blue Zones get their protein from beans and beans can make a very hearty stew or soup. Beans also help make a salad filling and satisfying. Nuts seem to play an important role and it doesn't matter what kind of nut. It might not be an apple a day that keeps the doctor away, rather a handful of nuts keeps the doctor away! Yum, I LOVE warmed nuts. What a treat to have every day!

Eating until you are 80% full means you can't wolf down your food. You need to eat slowly and savor your meal. This may take a conscious effort as Americans tend to eat quickly so we can get on to the next task. Blue zone residents enjoy their mealtime and usually eat with others. By conversing and laughing, you'll naturally slow down the pace of eating, and when you begin to feel full then stop eating. But you say you eat alone for lunch or dinner so you can't talk with others. Maybe yes and maybe no.

Consider calling a friend on the phone during a meal and let them know "I wanted to call and have dinner with you. I miss not seeing you." They'll be flattered and you will find that you will eat a LOT slower than sitting by yourself. Reading a magazine, news feed, or a book will also cause you to slow down between bites. You'll be focused on the story, and it is very difficult to stuff your mouth as you are reading.

Try timing yourself to see how fast you eat and then work to expand the amount of time you take to eat. You may be shocked that you eat a meal in less than 5 minutes. If so, expand it to 10 minutes, then 15 or 20 minutes. You'll avoid feeling stuffed and sluggish afterwards. If you are still hungry after eating, try having a warm cup of tea or coffee and it should do the trick! Wine isn't off-limits if it is consumed in moderation. This doesn't mean you can "save" your 1–2 glasses a day to binge on the weekend.

Okay, so we covered physical activity and diet. What's next? It is important to relieve stress and have a sense of community and a purpose in life. Over and over people in blue zones talk about how much they value the family and community. Americans have a very strong work ethic and some of us tend to be workaholics. The culture in the blue zones does not support being a workaholic.

They do work very hard, but balance it with rest, socialization, and stress-relieving activities. They take time to decompress, and this isn't sitting down to watch TV or look at their Facebook feed. I mean

REALLY decompress. I'm talking about sitting quietly to enjoy the sounds of nature, looking at the stars, or taking time to meditate. Some people enjoy journaling or keeping a gratitude diary. Even taking a bath with soft music can be an "Ahh" time for a busy girl!

Stress causes inflammation which destroys the body. Think about ways you can reduce stress. Some people take a social media break or reduce the number of "friends" they have. Are the 300 friends you have on Facebook really friends or just people you know? Do you really want to see what is going on in their lives or would you rather start living your own life? It is amazing how much time we can fritter away on our phones or computers.

To have a sense of community you need to engage in the community. When was the last time you talked to your neighbors? Are there ways to volunteer in the community? Is there a trash pickup day or a community get-together that you can join? Look for clubs or activities where you can join others. I love the Meet Up groups. There are a variety of groups that you can participate in. These range from getting together to listen to music, taste wine, do yoga, run together, play games, learn to meditate, etc. Most communities have some type of education or learning program. These include learning to knit, speak another language, learn about finances, astronomy, art appreciation, and more!

Another interesting concept in blue zones is having a small, tight-knit group of friends. The older folks have their "tribe" of friends who check in on them, encourage each other, and help when help is needed. This can relieve the "burden" on others as they all can relate to life as they are experiencing it. Many have developed very deep and strong bonds with each other. What is interesting is that these might not be lifelong friends, but rather other people in the same age group who met and decided to support each other.

Having a sense of spirituality is also important. Faith is strong and religion varies between blue zones. Attending a religious service, even as little as once a month, can extend your life. Hmm, what is going on here? People of faith tend to live healthier lives and take fewer risks. They engage in a community and the religious service serves as stress relief and time to decompress. There are periods of quiet reflection, and most churches or temples are very peaceful. Singing helps to relieve stress and produce feel-good hormones. There is a common set of values and a desire to be a good person. Overall, people who attend religious services experience a greater sense of self-awareness and self-esteem. You might say, "Yeah, but I'm not into organized religion." Well, maybe the typical Catholic or other formalized religious service doesn't appeal to you, but there are many other options out there. You'll most likely find a community that appeals to you and promotes a sense of inner peace. Give it a try, you don't have anything to lose and might gain several healthier years of life!

Another very strong commonality in the blue zones is putting family first. Americans are so busy trying to get ahead and provide for the family that we frequently forget to slow down and focus on the "now." How many times have you said, "Not now sweetie, I'm still working" or arrive home right before bedtime? In the blue zones, if a person could spend another hour working or that hour with their family, they ALWAYS choose the hour with the family! Whether they have children living at home, relatives within the same city or farther away, they prioritize family time.

You say that no one is living at home with you. You can still prioritize the family. You can call on the phone, put together a photo album (digital or printed photos) of memories, bake cookies to share or mail, start a project of knitting new scarves for the winter, memorialize life experiences by writing down your memories or creating audio stories that can be passed down. EVERYBODY loves to hear stories about themselves or remember fun experiences. It will mean so much and help to alleviate grief when someone passes away.

I gain comfort from using a coffee mug with a picture of myself, my sister, and my mom on it. I feel like I am having coffee with my mom who passed away many years ago. I dig out the old photo albums (remember when photos were developed from negatives) and relive my childhood through the memories evoked. Anyone at any age can create a memory keepsake that will be more meaningful than you can imagine to someone in the future.

This leads to another critical aspect of the centenarians, having a sense of purpose. The older folks in the blue zones have retired from the jobs they had when they were younger but still have a sense of purpose, a reason to get up in the morning. It may be to tend the garden. It could be to create a piece of art or do some woodworking. Maybe it is cooking favorite meals or treats for someone else. It could be learning something new.

Have you always wanted to learn a new language but never had the time to do it? Well, if you are retired you can master Spanish! It is great if you can engage a partner to learn something new. Wouldn't it be fun to learn a new language and speak to your friend only in that language? The first conversations would be very simple, but you can expand from "My name is Jane. What is yours?" to "I found a new recipe and made a very good stew that tasted great!" or "I found a great bargain at the store and bought a beautiful blue blouse."

For many people, retirement is a time to give back. Do you have any talents or areas of interest that could be helpful to others? If you were in business, is there a young business person who could benefit from being mentored by an expert? Would you like to help someone learn to read? Does the garden center or animal shelter need volunteers to help out? Women's organizations are always looking for volunteers to help support their members. Volunteer options abound in every community. Most positions are incredibly flexible with options from a few hours a month to several hours a week. Your contribution is greatly appreciated and most people find their work to be deeply satisfying.

A sense of purpose could be wanting to watch a grandchild grow up and get married. It could be wanting to read a book or watch a series that a friend recommended. People of any age will wither away if there is not a reason to get up or a purpose in their lives. If you know someone who is struggling with a sense of purpose, help them out. It could be asking them to share some recipes, make something (It could be as simple as place cards for a family get-together), or get them a pet. Cats do not require as much care, time, or energy as a dog and so many people find great joy and comfort from having a pet.

The lessons from the blue zones can be applied to any age. While not everyone will be able to embrace every aspect fully, begin to think about what you are already doing and how it can be improved or what you can get started doing. You might not want to live to 100 years old, but EVERYONE wants to live a life where you can be physically active, healthy, and have a sharp mind!

## Chase the Blues Away!

Everyone has a down day now and then. Maybe you didn't get enough sleep, or it is the fifth day of overcast skies and no sunshine, or it is deep into winter when it is cold and it gets dark at 4 pm. All you might want to do is go to bed and sleep! While that may be okay for a day, if you find that you are getting into a funk or feel like a cloud is following you then here are some measures to help you chase those blues away!

Physical exercise is probably the LAST thing you want to do, but it is one of the best things you can do! It gets your blood revving and releases endorphins (the feel-good hormones). But it is cold outside, and you don't want to go out. Okay, if going outside for a brisk walk won't work for you, how about a yoga session in front of the TV? You don't want to get in the car to drive to the gym? An at-home option is to put on some of your favorite tunes and dance for fifteen minutes. Boy, will you feel energized!

When I REALLY did not feel like exercising and just wanted to curl up on the couch with a glass of wine, I would pour the glass of wine and do some exercises at home with the glass of wine in front of me as my reward. Another great tip I learned from a colleague was to get on the treadmill "for just fifteen minutes." Over 90% of the time I stayed on for 45–60 minutes and felt so good afterwards! Over half the battle is just getting started doing something!

We've all heard the term "garbage in and garbage out" and it applies to our diet too. If you are eating highly processed, refined foods, drinking too much alcohol, or taking in a lot of sugar, you are not going to feel good. It takes a conscious effort to eat an apple versus a slice of apple pie.

Water can seem very boring until you really start hydrating yourself with it, then you'll become addicted to your 6–8 glasses a day! Most Americans are in a chronic state of dehydration. When you are dehydrated you can feel tired, hungry, and crabby. So, grab a glass of your favorite water (alkaline, mineral, sparkling, spring, or straight out of the tap) and drink the blues away!

Eating habits are hard to break. A habit develops after 6–8 weeks. If you've been eating a fast-food lunch for years, it is going to take some effort to change to turkey on whole wheat bread. Sugar can be especially difficult to limit. You can start by switching to lower-sugar options with the goal of avoiding foods with sugar added. You'll be surprised if you look at the label on "low fat" versions of your favorite foods. Many are LOADED with sugar or high-fructose corn syrup. Avoid the diet version and limit your full-fat portion. You'll be better off in the long run.

So many girls end their day with a couple of glasses of wine to relax. Moderation is the key. It can be very easy to go from two glasses to three or four a night. If this has been your "little treat" at the end of the day for a while, you'll need to find a substitute. Try switching to an alcohol-free refresher. I love low-sugar cranberry cocktail juice, either plain or with some sparkling water. It is tart and very refreshing! Drink it out of a wine glass, just leave out the wine! Experiment with mocktail recipes. If you love an old fashioned or pina colada, make it alcohol-free and enjoy the yummy taste of it.

During the winter months, if you are feeling like you can't wake up and are tired all day, you may have seasonal affective disorder (SAD). It is a disorder that is associated with shorter days and less sunlight. People feel tired, may crave carbohydrates, gain weight, and oversleep. If you feel that you are experiencing SAD, reach out to your healthcare practitioner. One intervention that may be suggested is light therapy. A blue light box can help alter your brain chemicals. It is used early in the morning. You don't look directly into the light but rather position it on your table or desk so you are bathed in it.

Other interventions may include talk therapy or anti-depressants. Everyone can benefit from getting outside (Hello, Vitamin D!), brightening up your home (open your blinds and let the light in), and laughing (watch your fave comedy show or movie). Pick one, two, or all interventions to chase those blues away and feel energized, positive, and full of life!

## Embrace a Sense of Spirituality

Happy, content people share a common trait, a sense of spirituality. Am I talking about religion? Not necessarily. Not everyone experiences spirituality in the same way. For some people, it can be a very deep religious faith that is followed, for others it could be sitting on a mountaintop and being awestruck by the wonder of the world. Simply put, spirituality means that you are focused on your purpose or meaning in life versus the material or physical aspects. For me, it is what grounds me and reminds me of what is really important in life. Of course, I'd love to win the lottery and receive ten million dollars.

But, even if that DID happen, if I didn't have a very strong sense of spirituality then my life would be shallow and empty.

So how does one nurture a sense of spirituality? And the key word here is NURTURE. It takes time and effort. You need time for reflection. Consciously say, "I am going to give myself X number of minutes." Even if it is only five minutes, you deserve it and need that time. And effort that you'll be able to disconnect from everything else going on in the world and forget about keeping up with the Joneses or comparing yourself to others.

If you need to, block the time out when you know it will be easier to keep your "date" with yourself. Some people like to reflect first thing in the morning before getting out of bed, others like to end the day with reflective time. For a VERY busy lady, think about turning off the radio in the car while driving or during your workout. You can make it work! Of course, if you do practice an organized religion then your weekly service is already built-in time for you, and for some people that is enough. However, many people find they need additional time.

Okay, you've found some time, now you want to know more about this nurturing business. I mentioned reflection. There are many ways to reflect, and you can explore different methods until you find one (or a few) that will work for you. There are gratitude journals, yoga, prayer, random acts of kindness, and counting your blessings.

I had a friend who looked for miracles and he found them every day. He changed my frame of reference and by paying attention, I can find them too. So can you! I always remember this when I am stuck in a traffic jam. These are usually caused by an auto accident, and some are fatal. Instead of getting irritated and angry about what could be a two-hour delay, I am thankful it was not me in the accident. I take that extra time to reflect on how easily it could have been me and how my life or the lives of my loved ones would change if I was the person in the accident. I like to take a few minutes to say a prayer for the accident victims and their families. Did someone say gratitude or "It's a miracle"?

Meditation is another VERY helpful method. Meditation can be guided or unguided where you focus on clearing your mind to get to a mindfulness state. Although, I've always thought of it as "mindlessness" as you need to totally clear your mind and that is VERY hard. Try meditating and not thinking of ANYTHING. Not easy!

The guided versions keep me focused and prevent those pesky thoughts such as what I need to get at the grocery store or what I need to do at work from sneaking in. YouTube is a great source for meditation. There are group meditation classes as well. Once you've established or strengthened a sense of spirituality, you'll feel an inner peacefulness that extends outwards. You'll attract others to your positive aura, and we all want to be bathed in peace and positivity!

## The Glass IS Half Full – The Power of Positivity!

One of the most significant realizations I had in my life came when I recognized that I had a choice as to how I viewed the world. Surprisingly, this occurred when I was a teenager. Teens tend to be ego-centric, moody, and negative. I remember one day when my mind was feeding into the "It's not fair" and "Why me?" thinking, I realized that I did not like myself. Negativity and victim-like thinking caused me anxiety and to have a pessimistic outlook. I decided to flip my thinking to a more positive outlook. Believe me, it can be easier said than done. Yet, if you consciously convert a negative thought to a positive one it can quickly become a habit. So how is this done?

You might need to enlist friends or family members to help you see the bright side initially. And yes, "things could be worse" is a thought to help spur you on to how things are actually better! Instead of lamenting about a two-hour flight delay (a definite downer), I am grateful that I can go on vacation. While it is still annoying, try to find some benefits, such as listening to a favorite podcast, calling a friend you've been meaning to talk to and have been putting off because she likes to talk for two hours, or just taking some deep breaths and trying to relax.

Did you encounter a very negative, crabby salesperson? Your immediate reaction may be to get defensive or angry – a natural response. Try to take a mental step back and think about how happy you are that you do not see the world in the same light or understand that this person may be going through some very trying times and may not even be aware of how off-putting they come across.

Another hurdle that can be difficult to overcome is comparing yourself to others. The "keeping up with the Joneses" syndrome. Social media feeds into this frame of reference. You see people having these wonderful lives, going to fun places, totally enjoying life, and with these fabulous bodies. While all this might be true, it could also be that your Facebook friends are feeling insecure and posting helps them to feel better. At times, the perfect life portrayed on Facebook covers up issues at home or with one's self-esteem. Photoshop can make anybody look smashing. Even if your friend does have a killer body, what does it take to get it? Is your friend starving herself or spending excessive amounts of time exercising? If she is lucky enough to have that "Oh my God" body without enormous sacrifices, then wish her well!

There will always be people better off than you and others who are living incredibly trying lives. Sometimes volunteering to help the less fortunate can be a real eye-opener and lead to a greater appreciation of your own life. Even if YOU are the one who is less fortunate or struggling, look at what you have been able to accomplish or the progress you are making. Did you learn to be a VERY creative cook on a tiny food budget? I once made this incredible spaghetti sauce from a can of tomato soup and some herbs!

Try to enjoy the things in life that cannot be bought: smelling honeysuckle on a walk, enjoying a bath after a busy day, a great sunrise or sunset, being grateful that your muscles ache after a day of hiking, or listening to a young child talking about how they see the world. An incredibly powerful four-minute video "Empathy: The Human Connection" was made by the Cleveland Clinic in 2013 and is posted on YouTube. I recommend you watch it, just be sure to have some tissues handy! It gives a look into the emotions and feelings of various people in a hospital setting. It left a monumental impression on me when I saw it in 2013 and is just as powerful today!

Everyone needs to find what grounds them. This is the prescription for when the "keeping up with the Joneses" thoughts come creeping back in. For some girls, a gratitude diary helps keep them grounded. Meditation is especially effective for many people. Other girls may find going to church or temple is the key. Figure out what works for you and use it to maintain your optimistic and compassionate view of the world.

Another tip is that positive, optimistic people are seen as much more attractive, with better personalities, and can dramatically change someone's life without even realizing it. That cranky sales lady that you did not snap back at, rather you might have said, "It seems like you might be having a bad day, I hope it gets better" could totally change her day knowing that someone cared. Letting the person behind you in line at checkout who has two items go ahead of you is an easy way to show kindness and you'll gain some "feel-good" emotions. Smiling kindly at the mother who has her hands full with a toddler at the store or church will help to reduce the embarrassment and frustration she is feeling dealing with a recalcitrant youngster.

The saying – "They will not remember what you said, but how you made them feel" —is so very true. Aim to be the person who sees life in a better way, is gracious, and strives to show kindness. You will be a shining star in this world where too many folks always want more and cannot see the wonderfulness in life.

## Me Time!

Something incredibly important and frequently neglected by women worldwide is "me time." So many women focus their energies on their jobs and loved ones and end up not having any time for themselves. Just like when you are on an airplane and they instruct you to put your oxygen mask on before helping others, we need to do the same. Women need some "me time" to decompress and recharge. I know, I know – you have a VERY busy life, a demanding job, children with various activities you need to take them to, etc. Well, if you don't take some "me time" (It doesn't have to be a lot, but more is better), then you will find that burning your candle at both ends will leave you with an extinguished flame or at the very least, a LOT less patience.

So, what is "me time"? It is time for you and you only to do WHATEVER you want! Oh, that sounds fabulous, but you say you cannot fit that into your schedule. Yes, you can! Remember it does not have to be a lot of time. Can you find 15 minutes once a day or every other day? Not everyone can give up 15 minutes of sleep in the morning, but how about 15 minutes before going to bed?

A common time zapper that many women, me included, do is not saying no to people. Why is this so hard? We want to be helpful, even if it is to our detriment. Instead of saying no, I might just say yes. What! Why did I say yes?! Or I may hedge by saying maybe. A MUCH better solution is to just say no or if that is too hard, then say no and include what you CAN do! "I'm sorry I can't help at the bake sale, can I make a cash donation?" or "No, I can't get together with the girls on Thursday night. I'd love to meet for coffee on a Saturday morning next month."

Where most women find it especially hard is saying no to our loved ones. Are you doing more than you should at home? Be honest with your family that you need some "me time" to maintain your mental health. Try dividing up responsibilities. If you do all the laundry, consider having your teen-aged children do their own. Even young children can fold and put away their own clothes. They will gain a sense of responsibility and likely enjoy contributing to the family.

Lowering your expectations can help too. Are you a stickler for how dishes are put in the dishwasher or placed in the cabinet? If you need to create "me time," allow other family members to do the dishes and put them away. Does it really matter if the fork tines are facing up in the dishwasher if the forks get cleaned and put away?

Are you living on your own and looking to find time? Do you really need to vacuum every other day? Could the dishes sit in the sink overnight? Think about how you can be more efficient. Could you prep your food for the week on Sunday to reduce the time it takes to make dinner each night? Weigh the pros and cons of doing your own household chores. Can the kid down the street cut your grass? How much is a cleaning lady, and could you use one every other week or once a month?

So, you've carved out some "me time," now what do you do? Sometimes it is hard for women to focus on themselves, although the choices are ENDLESS. You can spend some time reading a book, watching a chick flick, getting away from EVERYONE on your bike or hiking, meditating, starting a journal, taking up a hobby, joining that tennis league or exercise class at the gym, or engaging in luxury items like the fancy mani/pedi, massage, or weekend girls retreat.

Create a list and make choices based on the time you have and budget. You will be surprised at how much better you will feel and what a better mother, friend, lover, or workmate you will become. Treat this time as precious and make it a TOP priority. If you need to ditch something on your "to-do" list today, skip the dusting and keep your "me time." You'll be more radiant and brighten the day and guess what? No one will notice the dust when you are glowing!

# CONCLUSION

Thank you for reading my book! I hope you are ready to Wow the world! I'm sure you found many ideas to support your health, wellness, and let your inner and outer beauty shine forth! Whether you gained a few tips on how to improve your nutrition, sneak in some exercise to get toned, reduce your everyday stress, tell fine lines and wrinkles to stay away, create mesmerizing eyes, or dress to impress, I hope you realize it is a journey and are ready to start or continue it. Every woman is special and unique. My wish is for you to feel absolutely fantastic and show the world your incredible aura!

You might want to go back and make a list of your Must-Do and Fun-to-Try items. Share them with your friends and have a party to test out some of the ideas. Wouldn't it be fun to figure out who has warm or cool undertones and then help each other discover the best look for their figure and coloring? What a wonderful way to celebrate our differences and give support to our sisters.

How about bringing all those foundations you have and asking which one looks best under fluorescent lights and natural daylight? If that "buff" is not your color, it might look great on a friend! There are a number of ways you can share ideas and concepts with your friends and have a lot of laughs and enjoy becoming a better you!

I'm excited for you and am interested in your journey and experiences. I encourage you to stay in touch with me through www.marybeth newell.com. Be sure to sign up for my Tip of the Week. I'll send you a fun, quick golden nugget to keep you motivated and in the know. I also have a free e-book you can download with even more tips! Once you register, as I release additional books, you'll be the first to know and get a sneak peek of the new book. Stay tuned and stay beautiful!

# About the Author

 Mary-Beth Newell has had a lifelong love affair with nutrition, exercise, and inner and outer beauty. Her inquisitiveness led her to experiment and discover tips, tricks, and processes to defy nature. She is living proof you can look at least ten years younger while remaining genuine and happy. You might say she found the fountain of youth! As a registered nurse with a master's degree in science, she shares her wisdom, humor, and secrets with you! She resides in Sarasota, Florida with her "zoo" consisting of two energetic standard poodles and two talkative kitty cats.

Facebook: https://www.facebook.com/marybeth.newell.5
Instagram: https://www.instagram.com/marybethnewell/

www.ingramcontent.com/pod-product-compliance
Lightning Source LLC
Chambersburg PA
CBHW071021120626
46546CB00003B/1189